3

More Grammar Practice

HEINLE
CENGAGE Learning

Australia · Brazil · Japan · Korea · Mexico · Singapore · Spain · United Kingdom · United States

Contents

2

EXAMPLE	EXPLANATION
Emily **has liked** French movies for two years. She **has not enjoyed** English movies. **Has** she **seen** any Spanish movies?	Statement: *have / has* + past participle. Negative: *have / has* + *not* + past participle. *Yes / no* question: *Have / Has* + subject + past participle.
Marco **has been** at this school since 1999. He **has** always **wanted** to learn English.	The action started in the past and continues to the present: Now Past ···──►Future
He **has had** three exams this week. He **has met** several new friends so far.	The action repeats during a period of time that started in the past and continues to the present.
Has Marco ever **studied** another language? Marco **has studied** French, and he speaks it fairly well.	The action occurred at an indefinite time in the past. It still has importance to a present situation.

EXERCISE 1 Unscramble the words to make correct questions or statements.

Example: lived in Europe / I have / for five years
I have lived in Europe for five years.

1. abroad / traveled / have you ever

    _____

2. since she was 10 / she has been / interested in other cultures

    _____

3. to listen to / I have not / the Dutch language / had a chance

    _____

4. from home / have you ever / traveled / far away

    _____

5. English spelling / is difficult / have you ever thought that

    _____

EXERCISE 2 The verb in each of the following sentences is incorrect. Change the verb in each sentence to the present perfect tense.

Example: Many students from my country has studied abroad.
Many students from my country have studied abroad.

1. I always want to go to another country.

   _____

2. Are you ever go to another country?

   _____

3. She visit five countries so far.

   _____

4. Her brother have not travel to all seven continents.

   _____

EXERCISE 3 Use the present perfect tense of the verb in parentheses to complete each statement or question.

Example: Marco (always / dream) ____*has always dreamed*____ of studying English.

1. (ever / go) _____ Marco _____ to another language school?
2. He (study) _____ at two other English schools.
3. He (be) _____ here for a short time.
4. (find) _____ he _____ many new friends yet?
5. He (meet) _____ many new friends in the student dormitory.
6. (discover) _____ he _____ any useful ways to learn English?
7. Well, he (always / enjoy) _____ English movies.
8. He (not/ see) _____ many movies in English.
9. He (always / sing) _____ songs in English.
10. He (translate) _____ 10 French songs into English this year.
11. Marco (love) _____ music in any language since he was a child
12. (ever / go) _____ he _____ to a concert?
13. He (go) _____ to more than 20 concerts since the fall.
14. He (not / attend) _____ a play in English yet.

PRACTICE 2 — The Present Perfect Tense versus (vs.) the Simple Present Tense

EXAMPLE	EXPLANATION
I **am** in the United States now. I **have been** in the United States for two years.	The simple present refers only to the present time.
She **has** a car. She **has had** her car since March.	The present perfect with *for, since, always,* or *never* connects the past to the present:
I **love** my job. I **have** always **loved** my job.	Past Future Two years ago Now
I **don't like** tomatoes. I **have** never **liked** tomatoes.	

LANGUAGE NOTE: *For* and *since* are often used with the present perfect tense and the present perfect continuous tense. Use *for* when an action continued an amount of time:

    for 3 days   *for* an hour
    for weeks   *for* a long time

Use *since* when an action began at a specific time:

    since April   *since* he arrived
    since 8:30 a.m.   *since* that day

EXERCISE 1   Write Present next to the sentences that refer to the present. Write Present Perfect next to the sentences that connect the past to the present.

Example: She has worked in that restaurant since the beginning

of the year.   _Present Perfect_

1. He has a wonderful job in the city. _____

2. He is busy studying for his exams. _____

3. He has waited for three hours for the telephone call. _____

4. She has always wanted to travel around the world. _____

5. She has a friend who works in that supermarket. _____

6. Her brother works part time in the movie theater. _____

7. She has had three jobs since she started working last year. _____

8. I don't like to work in the summer. _____

9. You haven't had any luck for the past five years. _____

10. We have always liked her friends. _____

11. They never have any money. _____

12. It has never snowed since I moved here. _____

EXERCISE 2 Fill in the correct present perfect or simple present tense of the verb in parentheses.

Example: I (be) _____ *am* _____ in Rio de Janeiro right now.

1. I (be) _____ here since last week.

2. He (have) _____ a new bicycle.

3. He (have) _____ it for only one month so far.

4. She (call) _____ her mother every day.

5. She (call) _____ her father three times this week.

6. We (like) _____ this ice cream very much.

7. We (try) _____ all the flavors this summer.

8. You (always / try) _____ to learn languages since you were young.

9. You (never / like) _____ this city since you arrived here.

10. They (have) _____ a car since last year.

EXERCISE 3 Fill in each blank in the conversation with the simple present or the present perfect tense of the verb in parentheses.

Conversation 1

A: I see that you (**Example:** be) _____ *are* _____ interested in a part-time job.

B: Yes, I (1. be) _____ .

A: Well, we (2. like) _____ to talk to students who are motivated to work.

Conversation 2

A: I (3. always / want) _____ to be a doctor.

B: (4. be) _____ you sure that's the right career for you?

A: Yes, I (5. dream) _____ about it since I was a child.

B: (6. be) _____ you a good student? Doctors have to study hard!

Conversation 3

A: How is your new job?

B: Oh, I (7. love) _____ it. I (8. never / had) _____ a better job!

A: Really? Where (9. be) _____ your office? Maybe I should get a job there.

B: But you (10. never / want) _____ a permanent job.

PRACTICE 3 — The Present Perfect Continuous Tense

EXAMPLE	EXPLANATION
I **have been working** as a pilot for over 30 years.	The present perfect continuous tense = *have* or *has* +*been* + verb –*ing*.
He **has been living** in Paris for the past few years. He **has lived** in Paris for the past few years.	With some verbs we can use either the present perfect or present perfect continuous tense with actions that began in the past and continue to the present. There is very little difference in meaning.
Compare: He is working now. He **has been working** for the past 8 hours.	If the action began in the past and is happening right now, at this minute, use the present perfect continuous tense.
I have **always** loved to fly. I have **never** had another career.	Do not use the continuous form with *always* and *never*.

LANGUAGE NOTES:

1. We do not use a continuous tense with the following nonaction verbs:

believe	have	like	mean	prefer	seem
care	hear	love	need	remember	understand
cost	know	matter	own	see	want

2. *Have* and *think* can be action or nonaction verbs, depending on their meaning:
   I *have been thinking* about retirement. (think about = action verb)
   I *have* always *thought* that flying is exciting. (think that = nonaction verb)
   Tom *has been having* a good time with his cousins. (have = action verb)
   Tom *has had* many friends in school. (have = nonaction verb)

EXERCISE 1 Change each statement to a present perfect continuous tense sentence, using the information in parentheses next to each statement.

Example: I study English. (three years)
I have been studying English for three years.

1. She lives in an apartment with three friends. (since September)

2. I look for jobs on the Internet. (all day)

3. My brother teaches Spanish. (10 years)

4. The scientist works on the experiment. (for many years)

5. We study to play the guitar. (for two months)

_____

6. They look for a new apartment. (since 9:30 this morning)

_____

EXERCISE 2 Circle the correct underlined verb for each sentence using a nonaction verb.

Example: He (has been) / has been being at that company for a long time.

1. She has needed / has been needing to go to the dentist since her tooth broke.
2. The gift you gave me has mattered / has been mattering a lot to me.
3. You have been knowing / have known how to play the guitar for a long time.
4. They have seemed / have been seeming tired recently.
5. I have been owning / have owned two televisions in my life.
6. The doctor has been thinking / has thought about his patients today.
7. The students have wanted / have been wanting to take a vacation.
8. The tourists have studied / have been studying the history of the country.
9. Julia has been believing / has believed in life on other planets for many years.
10. I have never been having / have never had many bad dreams.

EXERCISE 3 Fill in each blank using the present perfect continuous tense. Use the present perfect tense with nonaction verbs.

Roberto (**Example:** work) _____has been working_____ at his new company as a sales

manager for more than a year. Recently he (1. travel) _____ in Europe.

He (2. be) _____ on a business trip for more than three weeks. He

(3. go) _____ on a lot of business trips these days, but he doesn't mind.

He (4. have) _____ the opportunity to see many countries.

Roberto (5. take on) _____ a lot of new responsibilities at his job.

For the last six months he (6. manage) _____ six new employees. He

(7. train) _____ them to get ready to meet customers. Also, he (8. do)

_____ some of his boss' work while she is on vacation. Even after work he

(9. volunteer) _____ to teach the new employees computer skills. Roberto

(10. always / think) _____ about other people more than himself.

The Present Perfect Tense vs. the Simple Past Tense

EXAMPLE	EXPLANATION
How long **have** you **had** your present car? I've **had** my present car for three months. How long **have** you **been working** there? I've **been working** there for two years.	Use *how long* and *for* with the present perfect or present perfect continuous tense to include the present.
How long **did** you **have** your last car? I **had** my last car for six years.	Use *how long* and *for* with the simple past tense when you are not including the present tense.
When did you **come** here to study? I **came** here a few months **ago**.	The simple past tense is used with questions that ask *when* and sentences that use *ago*. *Ago* is used after a time phrase and means *in the past*.
I **came** to this school in 1999. I **have been** at this school since 1999. I **have been studying** at this school since 1999.	Use the past tense to refer to a past action that does not continue. Use the present perfect (continuous) tense to show the continuation of an action from past to present.

LANGUAGE NOTE: Use *for* when an action has continued an amount of time (*for* three days, *for* an hour). Use *since* when an action has begun at a specific time (*since* April, *since* he arrived, *since* 8:30).

EXERCISE 1 Circle the correct verb tense. If both tenses are possible, circle both.

Example: How long (did she study) / has she studied last night?

1. How long has she been studying / did she study English when she was in high school?

2. She has been studying / studied English for five years.

3. When did he begin / has he begun working at the hospital?

4. He started / has started a month ago.

5. When did you visit / have you been visiting her?

6. I have been going / went at noon.

7. How long has she been driving / did she drive tonight?

8. She has driven / drove for five hours tonight.

9. She driven / drove for five hours tonight.

10. How long did you travel / have you traveled on your vacation last month?

11. I <u>traveled / have been traveling</u> for two weeks on my vacation last month.

12. When <u>did you return / have you returned</u> to work after vacation?

13. I <u>returned / have returned</u> to work at the end of last week.

14. They <u>ate / have eaten</u> everything in the refrigerator last night.

EXERCISE 2 Add the correct word from the list below. Write Ø (nothing) if no word is needed:
ago   since   for   when   how long

Example: _____*How long*_____ have you been studying English?

1. I have been studying English _____ four years.

2. _____ did your parents first visit Japan?

3. Three years _____ they visited Japan.

4. _____ has she known her best friend?

5. She has known her best friend _____ August 1993.

6. _____ did you watch TV last night?

7. I watched TV _____ an hour and a half.

8. _____ did you eat your breakfast?

9. I ate my breakfast _____ at seven o'clock this morning.

10. You haven't eaten anything _____ we ate dinner last night.

EXERCISE 3 Write a question in the simple past or present perfect tense for each of the following answers.

Example: *How long has she studied?* _____

She has studied for three hours.

1. _____

She came to this language school two months ago.

2. _____

She has been here for two months.

3. _____

She has made many new friends.

The Present Perfect Tense with Indefinite Past Time

We use the present perfect tense to refer to an action that occurred at an indefinite time in the past that still has importance to the present situation.

EXAMPLE	EXPLANATION
Has Daniel **ever** worked in a restaurant? No, he hasn't.	A question with *ever* asks about any time between the past and the present. Put *ever* between the subject and the main verb.
Has he found a job **yet**? No, not **yet**. Has his wife found a job **yet**? Yes, she has **already** found a job.	*Yet* and *already* refer to an indefinite time in the near past. There is an expectation that an activity took place a short time ago. *Yet* means *up to now*. *Already* means *before now*.
Has he had a lot of interviews **lately**? Has he seen a career counselor **recently**?	*Lately* and *recently* refer to an indefinite time in the near past; not long ago.
He has **just** finished having an interview.	*Just* means a short time ago.

LANGUAGE NOTE: We commonly use *yet* with questions and negative statements. Use *already* with questions and affirmative statements.

EXERCISE 1 Rewrite each statement or question with the word in parentheses.

Example: (ever) Have you been to Brazil?

Have you ever been to Brazil?

1. (recently) She hasn't done her homework.

   _____

2. (just) They have seen the new movie.

   _____

3. (already) I've seen the movie three times.

   _____

4. (yet) Has the school year ended?

   _____

5. (lately) I haven't seen your friend Thomas.

   _____

EXERCISE 2 Fill in the blanks in the conversations with *already, yet, lately, recently,* or *just.*

Conversation 1

A: Have you been looking for a job?

B: Yes, I have (**Example:**) _____*just*_____ finished school and have

(1) _____ started looking for a job.

A: I see. Have all your friends (2) _____ found jobs?

B: No, not (3) _____. Only my friend, David, has

(4) _____ found a job.

A: How long did it take him to find a job?

B: Not long. He (5) _____ finished an interview this morning

and was offered a job this afternoon!

Conversation 2

A: Hey, have you seen Serge?

B: No, not (1) _____. Why?

A: He promised me he would study with me for the exam.

B: He told me that he has (2) _____ studied for the exam.

A: Really? I haven't started studying (3) _____. Want to study with me?

B: No, sorry. I (4)_____ told Mary I'd study with her.

EXERCISE 3 Write a question with *Have you ever* and the words given for each exercise.

Example: study a foreign language other than English

Have you ever studied a foreign language other than English?

1. spend more than three months away from home

_____

2. have a part-time job

_____

3. use the Internet to find a job

_____

4. speak English at home

_____

5. travel around the world

_____

PRACTICE 6 The Present Perfect Continuous Tense with Ongoing Activities

EXAMPLE	EXPLANATION
Lisa **has been looking** for a new job lately. I **have been thinking** about taking a vacation recently. My English **has been improving**.	We use the present perfect continuous tense to show that an activity has been ongoing or repeated from a time in the near past to the present.

LANGUAGE NOTE: Remember, do not use the continuous form with nonaction verbs.

EXERCISE 1 Circle the better form of the verb to complete each sentence.

Example: I been / (have been) looking for a job for a long time.

1. She has been wanting / has wanted a new job since last year.
2. She has had / has been having several interviews in the past week.
3. I have been watching / watched the news recently.
4. I have been understanding / have understood the news in English recently.
5. For the past year I have owned / have been owning a big color TV.
6. I have been seeing / have seen the evening news every night.
7. They have been discussing / discussed politics over the last few days.
8. The store has been selling / has been sold international newspapers lately.

EXERCISE 2 Complete each sentence with the correct form of the verb *have*.

Example: She _____ *has* _____ been working on the computer all day.

1. You _____ been talking on the telephone for two hours.
2. He _____ been practicing piano for the past 20 minutes.
3. My athletic ability _____ been improving since last summer.
4. My friends _____ been eating dinner since 6:00 p.m.
5. The storm _____ been increasing since we arrived this morning.

EXERCISE 3 Fill in each blank with a noun phrase to make a true statement.

Example: _____The population_____ has been increasing.

1. _____ has been getting better.
2. _____ has been getting worse.
3. _____ has been improving.
4. _____ has been changing more and more.
5. _____ have been getting more dangerous.
6. _____ have been getting safer.

EXERCISE 4 Write statements using the present perfect continuous tense. Use *have* or *haven't*.

1. study hard / recently
   I have been studying hard recently.

2. improve my English / lately
   _____

3. make travel plans
   _____

4. meet friends for dinner
   _____

5. write letters to my relatives / lately
   _____

6. go to the movies / recently
   _____

7. do research on the Internet / recently
   _____

8. send e-mail messages to friends
   _____

9. make a lot of long-distance phone calls
   _____

10. spend time with my family
    _____

11. earn lots of money / recently
    _____

12. relax and take it easy / lately
    _____

PRACTICE 7 — The Present Perfect Tense with No Time Mentioned

EXAMPLE	EXPLANATION
I'm a pilot. People **have** often **asked** me how I became interested in flying. I **have lived** in many locations. I **have flown** to many cities.	Use the present perfect tense to talk about the past without any reference to time. The time is not important, not known, or not precise.
I **have studied** Portuguese and can use it in business. If you **have filled** the receptionist's position, please consider me for any other position in your company.	Use the present perfect tense without reference to time to show that the past is relevant to a present situation.

EXERCISE 1 Use the words below to write sentences in the present perfect tense.

Example: I / travel / to many places
I have traveled to many places.

1. you / read / many good books

2. they / sing / many songs

3. we / eat / several unusual dishes

4. he / play / tennis many times

5. she / meet / hundreds of people from around the world

6. the woman / run / two marathons

7. the movie star / own / many different kinds of cars

8. I / be / to the dentist's office too many times

9. my sister / live / in three countries

    _____

10. the ship / sail / the oceans of the world

    _____

11. you / spend / money at the department store

    _____

12. the instructor / look up / many English words in the dictionary

    _____

EXERCISE 2 Fill in each blank with the present perfect or the simple past tense of the verb in parentheses.

A. Sandy (**Example:** be) _____ *has been* _____ to many different countries. She (1. visit)

_____ six countries in Europe, three in Asia, and two in South America.

Last week she (2. go) _____ to New Zealand for the first time. She wrote

me a postcard and told me that she (3. see) _____ a kangaroo and that she

(4. pet) _____ a koala bear too.

B. Jerry (5. meet) _____ a lot of new friends in his English class. He

(6. meet) _____ two students from Argentina at the beginning of the year,

and he told me that they (7. invite) _____ him to go skiing there in the

winter. He (8. make) _____ plans last week to meet them during school

vacation. He (9. not / tell) _____ them that he (10. never / ski)

_____

C. I (11. study) _____ English and can use it to get a job. I (12. speak)

_____ with several people who (13. say) _____

that my English skills are quite good. I (14. ask) _____ friends in

English-speaking countries to give me advice. One friend from Ireland (15. call)

_____ me last night to tell me about a job in a restaurant in Dublin.

PRACTICE 8 — The Present Perfect Tense vs. the Present Perfect Continuous Tense with No Time

EXAMPLE	EXPLANATION
a. My teacher **has helped** me with my English. b. My friend **has been helping** me a lot. a. I **have decided** to travel around the world. b. I **have been planning** a trip. a. **Have** you **been** on a trip recently? b. **Have** you **been planning** a trip?	Examples (a) refer to a singular occurrence at an indefinite time in the past. Examples (b) refer to an ongoing activity.

 EXERCISE 1 Write **I** next to sentences that refer to *something that occurred at an Indefinite time in the past*. Write **O** next to sentences that refer to an *Ongoing* activity.

Example: My friend has been in a building that was shaken badly by an

earthquake. _____/_____

1. I have seen two good movies recently. _____

2. My friend has been speaking English to me a lot. _____

3. I have been waiting to see my best friend. _____

4. You've seen your family recently. _____

5. The little girl has lost her tooth. _____

6. You have been doing a lot of work. _____

7. I have been wondering about my future. _____

8. He has done his homework. _____

EXERCISE 2 Read each sentence; then check the statement that most closely agrees with the sentence.

Example: She was studying one hour ago. She is still studying now.

_____√_____ She has been studying.

_____ She has studied.

1. He has decided to go to England, France, and Germany for vacation.

_____ He has been deciding.

_____ He decided.

2. David worked in companies all over the world.

_____ He has been working.

_____ He has worked.

3. He was thinking about her all day yesterday. He is thinking about her now.

_____ He has been thinking about her.

_____ He thought about her.

4. He came up with a good solution to the problem.

_____ He has come up with a solution.

_____ He has been coming up with a solution.

EXERCISE 3 Change each of the following sentences and questions from a past activity to an ongoing activity.

Example: He has cooked almost every night.

He has been cooking almost every night.

1. She has helped me with my English homework.

_____

2. Have you practiced your English lately?

_____

3. Many people have watched the Olympic Games.

_____

4. They have traveled the world together.

_____

5. She has sailed her boat from Sydney to Hobart.

_____

6. Their parents have written them long letters.

_____

7. They have received postcards from around the world.

_____

8. Have you taken any English or American literature courses?

_____

PRACTICE **9** Passive and Active Voice

ACTIVE	PASSIVE
They **sell** tickets the day of the show.	Tickets **are sold** the day of the show.
Many people **saw** the movie *Titanic* last night.	The movie *Titanic* **was seen** by many people last night.
Shakespeare **wrote** the play *The Tempest*.	The play *The Tempest* **was written** by Shakespeare.

LANGUAGE NOTES:

1. The passive voice is created by using a form of *be* + the past participle. A passive verb is often followed by *by* + the person or thing doing or **performing** the action:

Subject	*Be*	*Past particple*	*By performer of action*
The movie	was	seen	by millions of people.

2. The active voice focuses on the performer of the action. In other words, the subject performs the action:

   My brother saw the movie *Titanic* six times.
   (The emphasis is on **My brother,** and he performs the action.)

   The passive voice focuses on the receiver of the action. The action is not performed by the subject of the sentence. The subject receives the action:

   The movie *Titanic* was seen by millions of people.
   (The emphasis is on **the movie *Titanic*,** but it is not the performer.)

 EXERCISE **1** Write *Active* if the sentence is active or *Passive* if the sentence is passive. Underline the <u>performer</u> of the action. In some cases, there is no performer.

Example: _____*Active*_____ <u>Millions of people</u> watch TV every night.

_____*Passive*_____ TV sets are purchased by <u>millions of people</u>.

1. _____ Many people have more than one TV in their home.
2. _____ Cable television is seen by people all over the world.
3. _____ People in many different countries watch the same TV shows.
4. _____ Many people use the Internet to shop.
5. _____ More and more people are drawn to the Internet's possibilities.
6. _____ The Internet is used every day by millions of people.
7. _____ Have you seen any good videos recently?
8. _____ The video has been rented.
9. _____ We were stopped by the police.
10. _____ The homework will be completed by the students tomorrow.

EXERCISE 2 Use the following words to write statements in the passive voice.

Example: (the patient / examine / by the doctor)

The patient is examined by the doctor.

1. (a book / write / by an author)

   _____

2. (an airplane / fly / by a pilot)

   _____

3. (a ballet / dance / by dancers)

   _____

4. (students / teach / by teachers)

   _____

5. (instruments / play / by musicians)

   _____

6. (buildings / build / by construction workers)

   _____

7. (Web sites / design / by the computer programmers)

   _____

8. (the language / learn / by the students)

   _____

9. (the fish / catch / by the fishermen)

   _____

10. (the delicious meal / prepare / the chef)

   _____

PRACTICE 10 The Passive Form with a Performer

TENSE	SUBJECT	*BE*	PAST PARTICIPLE	BY SOMEONE (OPTIONAL)
Simple Present	The movie	is	loved	by hundreds.
Present Continuous	The TV show	is being	watched	by millions.
Future	The TV show	will be	seen.	
Simple Past	The movie	was	seen	by my friends.
Past Continuous	The TV show	was being	watched	by the children.
Present Perfect	The TV show	has been	enjoyed.	
Modal	The movie	might be	seen	by many teenagers.

LANGUAGE NOTES:

1. The tense of *be* changes to fit the tense of the sentence.
2. Use the past participle with every tense in the passive voice:
   The papers were *filed* by the assistant.
3. An adverb can be placed between the auxiliary verb and the main verb:
   The ceremony is *usually* held in March.
4. Never use *do*, *does*, or *did* with the passive voice:
   The movie *wasn't* made in the United States. (**not:** The movie didn't made in the United States.)
   When *was* the movie made? (**not:** When did the movie made?)
5. If two verbs in the passive voice are connected with *and*, do not repeat *be*:
   The movie is *seen* and *loved* by millions of people.
6. After *by* the object pronoun is used:
   Active: She saw him.   *Passive:* He was seen by *her*.

EXERCISE 1 Fill in the blanks with the passive voice of the verb in parentheses, using the tense given.

Example: (simple past tense: *see*)

The movie *Titanic* _____was_____ _____seen_____ by millions

of people.

1.   (simple present: *show*)

Before a movie comes out, it _____ _____ to a big audience.

2.   (present perfect: *make*)

Many movies _____ _____ _____ about

the future.

3. (simple present: *think*)

The movie *Star Wars* _____ _____ to be one of the best

science fiction movies.

4. (simple past: *direct*)

The movie *Star Wars* _____ _____ by George Lucas.

5. (present perfect: *award*)

It _____ _____ _____ just about every movie

award that there is.

6. (simple present: *use*)

Home computers _____ _____ by many for work and

pleasure.

7. (simple past: *buy*)

Last year computers _____ _____ by many university

students.

8. (present perfect: *put*)

Assignments _____ _____ _____ on the

Internet by professors.

9. (simple past: *select*)

The best Internet Web sites _____ _____ by a committee of

university students.

EXERCISE 2 Change each of the following sentences from the active to the passive voice.
Keep the same verb tense.

Example: People in 12 countries watched the same television program.

The same television program was watched by people in 12 countries.

1. Young people all over the world can view the same programs.

_____

2. Both older people and younger people use the Internet.

_____

3. Many companies have created Internet Web sites.

_____

4. Many companies sell products over the Internet.

_____

5. A famous computer company president gave a speech about the Internet.

_____

6. Thousands of people listened to the speech.

_____

Practice 10   **23**

PRACTICE 11 Using the Active Voice Only

EXAMPLE	EXPLANATION
He **lived** in Japan for many years. He **became** an English teacher there. **Incorrect:** He **looks** the book. **Correct:** He **looks** at the book.	Some verbs are not used with the passive voice. These are verbs that have no object: happen go fall become be live sleep come look remain die seem work recover These are called *intransitive* verbs.
My brother *changed* as he got older. We *moved* to a new apartment. The plan *was changed* the next day. The furniture was *moved* to the other room by the workers.	The active voice is used with *change* and *move* when the action happens by itself. The passive voice is used with these verbs if someone causes the action to happen.
The car *stopped* at the corner. The car *was stopped* by the police.	The active voice is used with *start, stop, open,* and *close* even though the subject is not really the performer. The passive voice is used with these verbs if the performer is mentioned.

LANGUAGE NOTES:

1. *Have* is not usually used in the passive voice:
   Awkward: A good time *had been had* at the party.
2. We say *was / were born* (passive construction). *Die* is always an active verb:
   I *was born* in 1984.   Their grandmother *died* 10 years ago.

EXERCISE 1   Circle the verbs that are not used in the passive voice.

eat   (sleep)   come   go   have   born   work

die   look   see   watch   remain   catch   send

EXERCISE 2   For each pair of underlined verbs, circle the correct form of the verb.

Last year a friend from China (**Example:**) came / has come to visit me for a few weeks. We

(1) went / were gone to many places while she was here. She (2) saw / were seen many new things.

This was her first time in this country, and several unusual things (3) happened / were happened.

First, many people (4) were eating / eaten in the streets. She didn't understand why people

(5) had / were had snacks in the street. She (6) hearing / heard some people talking very loudly on

the train. She even saw a man steal a woman's wallet. The man (7) <u>stopped / was stopped</u> by the police. The wallet (8) <u>returned / was returned</u> to the woman.

She was also very surprised at the size of everything. She (9) <u>told / was told</u> by a Chinese friend before she came that it was a little like China here. By the end of her visit, she (10) <u>began / was begun</u> to feel more comfortable here. She (11) <u>seemed / was seemed</u> to enjoy it more. Overall, I think she (12) <u>enjoyed / was enjoyed</u> her visit very much.

EXERCISE 3 Which of the following sentences can be changed to the passive voice? Change those sentences. If the sentences cannot be changed, write *No change*.

Example: It happens all the time.
No change

1. She slept all morning.

   _____

2. Most students take the exam.

   _____

3. The professor changed the date and time of the exam.

   _____

4. The administration moved the class to another building.

   _____

5. The exam started at 8:00 a.m.

   _____

6. She opened her eyes at 9:30 to the sound of a knock.

   _____

7. She looked at the clock and remained in bed.

   _____

8. Her friends came into the room.

   _____

PRACTICE 12 Participles Used As Adjectives

PRESENT PARTICIPLE	PAST PARTICIPLE
We saw an **entertaining** movie.	The letters are in **sealed** envelopes.
Star Wars is an **exciting** movie.	We love **fried** chicken.
I bought new **drinking** glasses.	There was only one **broken** computer.
Star Wars has **amazing** visual effects.	I wasn't **bored** during the movie.

LANGUAGE NOTES:

1. A present participle is verb + *–ing*. A past participle is the third form of the verb (usually ending in *–ed* or *–en*). Both present participles and past participles can be used as adjectives.
2. A present participle shows that the noun it describes performs an action:
   A *caring* father is a father who cares for his child.
3. A past participle shows that the noun it describes receives an action:
   A *broken* window is a window that someone broke.

 EXERCISE 1 Circle the correct form of the participle.

Example: That was an amazed / (amazing) movie.

1. We ate the boiling / boiled eggs for dinner.
2. We had a terrified / terrifying car ride through the mountains.
3. I was exhausting / exhausted when it was over.
4. The movies certainly weren't boring / bored.
5. The disappointed / disappointing children didn't like the cartoons on TV.
6. I received some disappointing / disappointed grades.
7. The annoyed / annoying uncle thought the children were too noisy.

EXERCISE 2 Write two sentences following each sentence given. Use a present participle in the first sentence and a past participle in the second sentence.

Example: The new shopping mall excites me.
The new shopping mall is exciting.
I am excited about the new shopping mall.

1. The TV show bores me.

_____

_____

2. The museum interests the students.

   _____

   _____

3. The musical play entertains us.

   _____

   _____

4. The children charm their parents.

   _____

   _____

5. The story inspires the patients in the hospital.

   _____

   _____

EXERCISE 3 Unscramble the words in each exercise to make a correct sentence or question.

Example: actor / is / he / entertaining / an

He is an entertaining actor.

1. ever / you / been / have / in acting / interested

   _____?

2. ate / fried / the / we / chicken / all of

   _____.

3. worried / their / mother / is

   _____?

4. children / to bed / go / tired / early

   _____.

5. boring / the whole / stayed / to see / I / movie

   _____.

6. by horror movies / you / terrified / are

   _____?

7. exciting / lately / any / movies / seen / you / have

   _____?

8. socks / look / those / worn / ragged / and

   _____.

9. two / in / the / are / there / eggs / beaten / recipe

   _____.

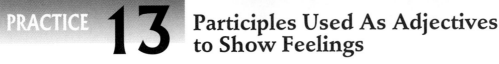

PRACTICE 13 Participles Used As Adjectives to Show Feelings

For some verbs both the present and the past participle can be used as adjectives.

	PRESENT PARTICIPLE	PAST PARTICIPLE
Movies entertain people.	Movies are **entertaining.**	People are **entertained.**
Chaplin's movies interest us.	Chaplin's movies are **interesting.**	We are **interested** in Chaplin's movies.

LANGUAGE NOTES:

1. A present participle shows the cause of a feeling. The subject is described:
   The movie bored me. ⟶ The movie was *boring*.
2. A past participle describes the receiver of a feeling:
   The movie *bored* the audience. ⟶ Some people were *bored*.
   The *bored* people got up and left.
3. A person can cause a feeling in others or he can receive a feeling:
   Chaplin had an *interesting* life.
   I am *interested* in Chaplin.
4. An object doesn't have feelings, so a past participle cannot be used to describe an object:
   The book is *interesting*.   (never *interested*)

EXERCISE 1 Fill in each blank with the correct participle (present or past) of the verb in parentheses.

Example: It was a long and (exhaust) _____*exhausting*_____ day.

1. She just read a book that she was (interest) _____ in.

2. She told me it was the most (interest) _____ book she has ever read.

3. She made a silly mistake, and now she is (embarrass) _____.

4. When she heard the (disappoint) _____ news, she called her friend.

5. The mystery was very (puzzle) _____ to the detectives.

6. The dog had a (puzzle) _____ look on his face.

7. Sometimes I find learning English to be (frustrate) _____.

8. I don't like being a (frustrate) _____ learner.

9. People learn better when they are (relax) _____.

10. I am (convince) _____ that your advice is the best.

11. I thought the news was (surprise) _____.

12. It seems that we are (amuse) _____ every day in class.

Write two new sentences using forms of the underlined word. Describe the subject. Then describe the object. Keep the same verb tense.

Example: The long airplane ride <u>exhausted</u> everyone.

The long airplane ride was exhausting.

Everyone was exhausted.

1. The unsolved mystery <u>puzzles</u> the nation.

   _____

   _____

2. The huge celebration meal <u>satisfied</u> the family.

   _____

   _____

3. The buzzing bees <u>annoy</u> the children.

   _____

   _____

4. The baseball game <u>excited</u> the fans from both teams.

   _____

   _____

5. The thunder and lightening <u>terrifies</u> the campers in the tents.

   _____

   _____

6. The magician's tricks <u>amazed</u> the audience.

   _____

   _____

7. The sudden storm <u>surprises</u> the boaters.

   _____

   _____

8. The sports competition <u>tires</u> all of the athletes.

   _____

   _____

9. The loud noises <u>shock</u> us.

   _____

   _____

Participles Used As Adjectives to Show Feelings

PRACTICE 14 The Past Perfect Tense

EXAMPLE	USES OF THE PAST PERFECT
We **had seen** the movie before.	Past perfect = *had* + past participle.
By the time the rescue ship arrived, the *Titanic* **had** alrcady **gone** down.	To show that something happened before a specific date, time, or event.
When people got on the lifeboats, the rescue ship **hadn't arrived** yet.	To show that something happened or didn't happen before the verb in the *when* clause.
There was a lot of ice in the water because the previous winter **had been** unusually mild in the Arctic.	After *because*, to show a prior reason.
The captain didn't realize how close his ship **had come** to the iceberg.	In a noun clause, when the main verb is past.
The passengers in third class were emigrants who **had left** behind their old way of life.	In a *who / that / which* clause, to show a prior action.
Many emigrants on the *Titanic* **had** never **left** their homelands before.	With *never . . . before*, in relation to a past time.
The ship **had been** at sea for five days when it hit an iceberg.	With *for*, to show the duration of an earlier past action.

EXERCISE 1 Complete the sentences with the past perfect tense of the verb in parentheses.

Example: I couldn't buy something to eat because I (forget) _____*had forgotten*_____ my wallet.

1. She didn't know the words to the song because she (never / hear) _____ it.

2. When they arrived at the theater, the movie (already / start) _____.

3. They (be) _____ on vacation for one week when they arrived in Paris.

4. By the time he called the fire department, his house (burn) _____ to the ground.

5. The team was made up of friends who (play) _____ together at the university.

6. By the end of the school semester, I (pass) _____ all of my exams.

7. She couldn't call her friend because she (lose) _____ his phone number.

8. She (just / reach) _____ home when it started to rain.

9. She (never / taste) _____ Japanese food before she went to Japan.

10. He (already / lose) _____ his glasses when he searched his backpack.

11. By the time the man left his house, the mall (already / close) _____ .

12. As he walked in the door, I (just / finish) _____ reading my novel.

13. When I opened the refrigerator, the milk (be) _____ there for a month.

14. I forgot to lock my house because I (leave) _____ quickly this morning.

15. The people who (arrive) _____ early left by 8:00 p.m.

EXERCISE 2   Fill in information about your own life and about people you know using the past perfect tense.

1. I had *finished elementary school* _____ by 1990.

2. I had never _____ before high school.

3. By 2000, I had already _____ .

4. Before last month I hadn't _____ because I was afraid.

5. My teacher had _____ before class ended.

6. By the time I finished my classwork, _____ .

PRACTICE 15   The Past Perfect Continuous Tense

EXAMPLE	EXPLANATION
The *Titanic* **had been traveling** for five days when it sank.	The past perfect continuous = *had + been + verb –ing*.
Some people **had been rowing** lifeboats for several hours by the time the rescue ship arrived.	The past perfect continuous tense is used to show the duration of a continuous action that was completed before another past action.

LANGUAGE NOTE: *Remember:* Do not use the continuous form with nonaction verbs.

EXERCISE 1   Underline the past perfect continuous tense in the following passage.

When he arrived in New Zealand to study English, he had been studying English for several years in his country. He had been going to a small language school near his home. He had liked the school, but he was tired of the same daily routine. He had been getting up at 7:00 a.m. every day, and he had been going to bed at 10:00 p.m. every night. For the past several years, he had been spending most of his free time studying. Since the spring, he had been feeling bored. At least since the summer he had been playing soccer on a neighborhood team. That gave him something to do. He had been planning to take a long trip in the summer, but his plans fell through at the last minute. Just before he started school this fall, his parents told him he could go to New Zealand. He had been dreaming about going to New Zealand for a long time. Now his dream had come true.

EXERCISE 2   Identify which part of each sentence happened first by writing **1** above it, and which part happened second by writing **2** above it.

                                   2   1

Example: Before she changed to biology   she had been studying chemistry for two years.

1. She had been studying English for 10 years   when she entered the university.

2. They had been taking piano lessons for five years   when they appeared in concert.

3. By the time they began watering the plants,   the plants had already started to die.

4. When the music stopped,   she had been dancing.

5. By the time the race finished,   she had been running for more than three hours.

6. He had been working at the company for more than 25 years   when he retired.

7. <u>When the bus finally arrived,</u> <u>the people had been waiting for over an hour.</u>

8. <u>I had been playing tennis for three hours</u> <u>when I decided to quit.</u>

9. <u>By the time I reached the summit,</u> <u>I had been climbing the mountain for six hours.</u>

10. <u>When I passed in my test,</u> <u>most students had already starting leaving the room.</u>

EXERCISE 3 Complete the following sentences with the past perfect continuous tense.

Example: They (fly) _____*had been flying*_____ for fifteen hours when the plane landed.

1. He (study) _____ English for five years when he arrived here.

2. The runners (run) _____ for 30 minutes when the race ended.

3. My father (work) _____ for three years when he met my mother.

4. It (only / rain) _____ for one hour when the rainbow appeared.

5. He (live) _____ in Tokyo when the accident occurred.

6. I (think) _____ of calling my friend when she called me.

7. She (write) _____ for three hours when she took a break.

8. She (read) _____ when the lights went out.

9. I (play) _____ the violin for 20 years when I joined the symphony.

10. We (plan) _____ a surprise party for her when she walked in.

11. When we woke you, you (dream) _____ .

12. When the tree fell over, the wind (blow) _____ for hours.

EXERCISE 4 Complete each sentence about yourself with the past perfect continuous tense.

Example: Yesterday, _____*I had been sleeping*_____ when my neighbor knocked on the door.

1. When the phone rang, I _____ .

2. I _____ when I decided to study English.

3. When I turned the TV off, I _____ .

PRACTICE 16 — The Past Perfect (Continuous) Tense or the Present Perfect (Continuous) Tense

EXAMPLE	EXPLANATION
When the passengers were rescued, they **had been rowing** for three hours.	The past perfect continuous tense is used to show that a continuous past action occurred before another past action.
The captain **had received** several warnings by the time he saw the iceberg.	The past perfect tense is used to show that a single action or a repeated action occurred before another past action.
We are talking about the movie *Titanic* now. We **have been talking** about it for 15 minutes.	The present perfect continuous tense is used to show that a continuous action occurred before the present time.
I **have seen** the movie *Titanic* several times.	The present perfect tense is used to show that a single action or a repeated action occurred before the present time.

LANGUAGE NOTE: The past perfect tense is used when we look back from a time in the past. The present perfect tense is used when we look back from the present time. The past perfect and the present perfect tense cannot be used interchangeably.

EXERCISE 1 Find the mistake in the underlined portion of each sentence. Rewrite the sentence correctly.

Example: By the time I got to the restaurant, my friend <u>waited</u> one hour.
By the time I got to the restaurant, my friend had been waiting for one hour.

1. I <u>have been seeing</u> my favorite movie hundreds of times.

   _____

2. <u>Had you ever been going</u> to the new shopping mall?

   _____

3. We are discussing the book. We <u>have discussed</u> it for three hours.

   _____

4. He <u>has called</u> her several times by the time he finally reached her.

   _____

5. When she finally passed the exam, she <u>has been studying</u> for over six months.

   _____

6. They <u>have been visiting</u> Tokyo many times.

   _____

7. It's now five o'clock. They <u>have been played</u> tennis for two hours.

   _____

8. She couldn't pay for her dinner because she <u>had been losing</u> her wallet.

   _____

9. How many times <u>have you sailing</u> on the ocean?

   _____

EXERCISE 2 Fill in each blank with the present perfect, present perfect continuous, past perfect, or the past perfect continuous tense of the verb in parentheses.

Example: She (be) _____*has been*_____ to Thailand six times.

1. When he finally hung up, we (talk) _____ for three hours.

2. She is living abroad now. She (live) _____ abroad for two years.

3. They (hear) _____ the thunder for an hour before the storm began.

4. They (see) _____ the movie *Titanic* more than 20 times!

5. He (study) _____ all night when his friends found him asleep.

6. He has a new job now. He (work) _____ there for seven months.

7. The author (write) _____ 17 children's books.

8. The singer (sing) _____ for 15 years by the year 2000.

9. It's noon. We (play) _____ basketball for two hours.

10. They (visit) _____ me many times.

11. When we finally finished, we (paint) _____ the room for four hours.

12. By the time I got home last night, I (walk) _____ for two hours.

13. I (call) _____ several times, but your phone is always busy.

14. We are ready now, and we (be) _____ ready for the past 15 minutes.

15. It's very late now. They (wait) _____ for a long time.

16. By the time she graduated, she (attend) _____ the university for five years.

PRACTICE 17 The Past Continuous Tense

EXAMPLE	EXPLANATION
What **were** you **doing** at 11:00 last night? I **was** not **sleeping**. I **was studying**.	The past continuous tense shows what was in progress at a specific past time.
Mr. Jones **was traveling** to Australia when the ship **sank**. While the ship **was sinking**, people **cried** for help.	We use the past continuous tense together with the simple past tense to show the relationship of a longer past action to a shorter past action.
We **were traveling** around the world. We **were attending** school.	In telling a story, the past continuous tense is used to describe a scene before the main action occurred.
They **were going to** go out for dinner, but their favorite restaurant was closed.	*Was / were going to* is used to show that a past intention was not carried out.

LANGUAGE NOTES:

1. If the time clause precedes the main clause, separate the two clauses with a comma:
   The *Titanic* was crossing the Atlantic Ocean when it sank. (No comma)
   When the *Titanic* sank, it was crossing the Atlantic Ocean. (Comma)
2. *While* is used with a past continuous verb. *When* is used with the simple past tense.
   Compare:
   While they were waiting for him, the movie started.
   They were waiting for him *when* the movie started.
3. *As* and *while* have the same meaning.

EXERCISE 1 Read the events of John's day yesterday, then complete the sentences. Use the past continuous tense.

8:00 a.m.	got ready for school	4:00 p.m.	went home
9:00 a.m.	went to school	5:00 p.m.	listened to music
10:00 a.m.	studied English	6:00 p.m.	fixed dinner
11:00 a.m.	wrote a research paper	7:00 p.m.	did homework
12:00 noon	ate lunch	10:00 p.m.	watched television
12:30 p.m.	talked with friends	11:00 p.m.	went to bed
2:00 p.m.	met with teacher		

Example: At 2:00 p.m. *John was meeting with his teacher.*

1. At 8:00 a.m. _____

2. At 6:00 p.m. _____

3. At noon _____

4.   _____ at 5:00 p.m.

5.   At 11:00 a.m. _____

6.   At 10:00 p.m. _____

7.   _____ at 10:00 a.m.

8.   At 11:00 p.m. _____

9.   At 2:00 p.m. _____

10. At 7:00 p.m. _____

EXERCISE 2 Fill in each blank with the simple past or the past continuous tense of the verb in parentheses.

Example: I was so hungry I (eat) _____*ate*_____ everything on my plate.

1.   The plane (take off) _____ for Venezuela on time.

2.   They (watch) _____ the World Cup soccer matches when the phone rang.

3.   It (snow) _____ very hard when they started down the mountain.

4.   They (be) _____ in a big group.

5.   While they (ski) _____, it continued to snow.

6.   They (go) _____ to stop, but they decided to keep skiing.

7.   Everyone (enjoy) _____ himself.

8.   All of the trees along the trails (look) _____ beautiful.

9.   It was still snowing when they (stop) _____ for lunch.

10. It (rain) _____ when they went out for a walk.

EXERCISE 3 Complete each of the following sentences. Use the past continuous tense.

Example: *She was working on her composition*___ when I got home yesterday.

1.   _____ as I was leaving the house.

2.   The students started to complain while _____

3.   As the teacher handed out papers, _____

4.   What was I doing at 8:00 p.m. last night? I _____

5.   Yesterday morning I _____

PRACTICE 18 Comparison of Past Tenses

EXAMPLE	TENSE
I **lived** in my country until 1997. The ship **left** England on August 5, 1993.	The **simple past** tense does not show a relationship to another past action.
I **was living** in Greece when I received permission to come here. She **was crossing** the street when the bus almost hit her.	The **past continuous** tense shows that something was in progress at a specific time in the past.
I **have been** here since 1998. People **have been** interested in dinosaurs for over a hundred years.	The **present perfect** tense uses the present time as the starting point and looks back.
I **have been living** here since 1998. We **have been talking** about that movie for several days.	The **present perfect continuous** tense uses the present time as the starting point and looks back at a continuous action that is still happening.
When I got permission to come here, I **had been** in Greece for 11 months. By the time the band started to play, most people **had** already **eaten** dinner.	The **past perfect** tense shows the relationship of a past action to an earlier past action.
When I got permission to come here, I **had been living** in Greece for 11 months. My family **had been traveling** for nearly 24 hours when their plane landed.	The **past perfect continuous** tense uses a past time as the starting point and looks back at a continuous action that was still happening.

EXERCISE 1 Identify the underlined verb tense in each sentence. Write *simple past, past continuous, present perfect, present perfect continuous, past perfect,* or *past perfect continuous.*

Example: She <u>had been traveling</u> for three months when she finished her trip.

past perfect continuous

1. They <u>studied</u> English until the year 2000. _____

2. I <u>had not eaten</u> all day when she offered me the sandwich. _____

3. They <u>have been</u> friends since childhood. _____

4. I <u>was watching</u> TV when I heard the news. _____

5. He <u>has been studying</u> at a language institute for six months. _____

6. She <u>had been writing</u> her graduate thesis when the war broke out.

   _____

7. My friends <u>came</u> to visit me last Friday night.   _____

8. I <u>was cooking</u> dinner when they arrived.   _____

9. They <u>have been living</u> nearby since September.   _____

10. I <u>have lived</u> in this neighborhood for four years.   _____

EXERCISE 2 Complete each sentence with the correct form of the verb in parentheses.

Example: When they stopped by to visit, I (read) _____*was reading*_____ a book.

1. My friends (live) _____ in Africa before they moved to China.

2. He (fly) _____ on an airplane more than a hundred times.

3. The summer after she finished school, she (take) _____ a trip.

4. By the time she returned home, she (visit) _____ classmates in over
   six countries.

5. Everyone (hear) _____ about the accident before the news was
   announced on the radio.

6. Many people (die) _____ in the earthquake.

7. Her father (work) _____ for the same company for over 35 years.

8. They (watch) _____ four videos last night.

9. By the time they sent a letter to their friend, she (return) _____ home.

10. They (use) _____ the Internet every day this week.

EXERCISE 3 Fill in each blank with the correct tense of the verb in parentheses.

   Last night I (**Example:** get) _____*got*_____ home very late. I (1. work)

_____ late, and then I (2. go) _____ to a baseball

game. I (3. not / saw) _____ a baseball game since I was ten years old. By

the time my friend arrived, I (4. wait) _____ for almost an hour. By the time

we got to our seats, the game (5. go on) _____ for an hour or so. Someone

(6. sit) _____ in our seats when we got to them, so we had to ask them

to move.

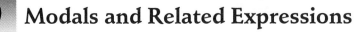

PRACTICE 19 Modals and Related Expressions

EXAMPLE	EXPLANATION
She **should** leave. (advice) She **must** leave. (necessity) She **migh**t leave. (possibility)	A modal adds meaning to the verb that follows it.
You **should** leave now. You **should not** leave now. **Should** you leave now?	The base form of the verb follows a modal. To form the negative, put *not* after the modal. To form a *yes / no* question, move the modal before the subject noun or pronoun.
A pen **should be used** for the test.	A modal can be used in passive voice: modal + *be* + past participle.
He **must** go to court = He **has to** go to court.	The following expressions are like modals in meaning: *have to, have got to, be able to, be supposed to, be allowed to, had better, ought to.*

LANGUAGE NOTES:
1. Don't use an infinitive after a modal.
2. Modals never have an *–s, –ed,* or *–ing* ending.
3. Don't use two modals together:
   You *will have to* go to court.   **Not:** You will must go to court.
4. *Shall* is more common in British English than in American English:
   British English: I *shall* see you tomorrow.
   American English: I *will* see you tomorrow.

EXERCISE 1 Circle the correct underlined portion of the sentence.

Example: She should stopped / (should stop) studying.

1. He <u>must be</u> / <u>must to be</u> gone.

2. They <u>might leaving</u> / <u>might leave</u> early.

3. He <u>must has to be</u> / <u>has to be</u> on time.

4. You <u>should being</u> / <u>should be</u> early.

5. We <u>are allowed to</u> / <u>are allow to</u> enter the building.

6. I <u>ought to</u> / <u>ought</u> wash the dishes right now.

7. He <u>should had better</u> / <u>had better</u> do it.

8. I <u>can</u> / <u>can able to</u> speak English well.

9. He <u>is being supposed to</u> / <u>is supposed to</u> visit me.

10. She <u>should leave not</u> / <u>should not leave</u> at this time.

EXERCISE 2 Answer each question using the modals and words in parentheses.

Example: Should we finish our homework now?

(yes / should)   *Yes, you should finish your homework now.*

1. Do I have to eat vegetables every day?

   (yes / must) _____

2. When does she have to leave?

   (might / tomorrow) _____

3. Will you go tomorrow?

   (no / might / not) _____

4. Do you think I have to study for the chemistry exam?

   (yes / had better) _____

5. Are you allowed to drive quickly in this city?

   (no / be allowed to / not) _____

6. Should I talk to my professor privately about my bad test score?

   (yes / ought to) _____

EXERCISE 3 The following sentences are all passive. Write the words and phrases in the correct order.

Example: might / done / the cleaning / by Friday / be
   The cleaning might be done by Friday.

1. be / as soon as possible / written / the letter / should

   _____

2. must / you / finished / with your school year / be / by now

   _____

3. ridden / the bicycle / be / very slowly / should / by the child

   _____

4. be / completed / my project / might / by next week

   _____

5. must / by the nurses / assisted / the patients / be

   _____

PRACTICE 20 *Must Not and Not Have To*

EXAMPLE	EXPLANATION
You **must not** lie in court.	Prohibition: This is against the law or rules.
You **don't have to** attend the meeting if you don't want to.	It is not necessary, not required, not expected. It is optional.
The student **doesn't have to** live in a dormitory.	

LANGUAGE NOTE: In affirmative statements, *have to* and *must* have a similar meaning. *Must* sounds more formal and is more for legal and urgent situations. In negative statements, *must not* and *not have to* have very different meanings.

EXERCISE 1 Write *R* if the rule is required. Write *O* if the rule is optional.

Example: ____R____ The sign says you must not enter the school before 8:00 a.m.

1. _____ You don't have to follow a lot of rules.
2. _____ You must not drive without a license.
3. _____ You don't have to wear formal clothes.
4. _____ If a book is overdue, you don't have to pay a fine.
5. _____ You must attend class on Friday to pass the course.
6. _____ We don't have to bring our books to class every day.
7. _____ We must not talk during tests.
8. _____ The students don't have to give presentations in front of the class.
9. _____ Teachers don't have to teach at night.
10. _____ You must come to class with your notebook and a pencil.

EXERCISE 2 Complete each sentence with *doesn't / don't have to* or *must not*.

At the private school there are many strict rules about clothes and dormitory life. There are

many things that students (**Example**) _____*must not*_____ do or they will be asked to

leave the school. They (1) _____ wear jackets and ties to class, but they

(2) _____ wear torn clothing. They (3) _____ wear

shorts or earrings either. They (4) _____ keep their hair very short, but they

(5) _____ have beards or mustaches.

42 Practice 20

In the dorms they (6) _____ make loud noise after 9:00 p.m.

They (7) _____ go to bed early, but they have to be in their rooms.

They (8) _____ leave their rooms without permission after 9:00 p.m.,

but on Saturdays they (9) _____ be in their rooms until 11:00 p.m.

In general, the students (10) _____ be supervised in the

library, but they (11) _____ disturb other students. Students

(12) _____ bring radios or CD players into the library. They

(13) _____ remain completely silent. For example, students may speak

quietly with other students or instructors. The librarian (14) _____

speak sternly to the students most of the time because they follow the rules.

EXERCISE 3 Write sentences about the rules at your school. Use one of these modals: *have to, must,* or *don't have to,* or *must not* in each sentence.

Example: sign in every day

I don't have to sign in every day.

1. call if you're going to miss class

   _____

2. be quiet during class

   _____

3. attend a certain number of classes a term

   _____

4. buy your own textbooks

   _____

5. eat lunch at school

   _____

6. leave cell phones off during class

   _____

7. wear formal clothes every day

   _____

8. study every night

   _____

Practice 20   43

PRACTICE 21 Comparing Negative Modals

EXAMPLE	EXPLANATION
You **don't have to** be a member of the club to use the swimming pool.	It's not necessary.
You **shouldn't** give strange callers your credit card number.	It's a bad idea.
Advertisers **cannot** place ads in magazines for children under 12. They **may not** place ads in magazines for children under 12.	It's prohibited. *Cannot* is written as one word.
You **must not** talk during the test.	It's prohibited. (official tone)
You **are not supposed to** talk during the test.	This is a reminder of a rule. (unofficial tone)
You**'d (had) better not** arrive late for the exam, or you won't have time to finish it.	This is a warning. A negative consequence is stated or implied.

EXERCISE 1   Match the modal in each sentence with its meaning.

Sentences

Example: You are not supposed to return
           books late. ___d___

1. You don't have to attend the party. _____
2. You shouldn't go out late alone. _____
3. You'd better do your homework. _____
4. You must not let your dog in the building. _____
5. Children under 18 cannot attend. _____

Meaning

a. It's a bad idea.

b. This is a warning.

c. It's prohibited.

d. This is a reminder of a rule.

e. It's prohibited (official tone).

f. It's not necessary.

EXERCISE 2   Circle the better modal expression to complete each sentence.

Example: You ('d better not) / shouldn't miss the practice or you won't be able to play
           in the game.

1. You <u>must not / don't have to</u> bring an ID. They have all the necessary information.

2. Soccer players <u>are not supposed to / don't have to</u> wear their uniforms during practice. They can use their own athletic clothes.

3. Salesmen <u>cannot / don't have to</u> enter private buildings.

4. Students <u>shouldn't / may not</u> use the student lounge for parties. It's not allowed.

5. They <u>shouldn't / are not supposed to</u> have visitors in the dorm after 9:00 p.m. The rule is in the handbook.

6. You <u>shouldn't / must not</u> put off doing your homework until the last minute. It's a bad habit.

7. The children <u>cannot / don't have to</u> eat any more cookies tonight. I don't want them to get sick.

8. Sam <u>is not supposed to / had better not</u> forget his wallet this time because I'm not paying for him!

9. Sheila <u>must not / shouldn't</u> tell lies or she'll end up with no friends.

10. People without tickets <u>had better not / may not</u> enter the security area.

11. You <u>shouldn't / must not</u> bring babies into movie theaters. Their crying disturbs people.

12. You <u>don't have to / may not</u> go to an English-speaking country to learn English.

13. The final research report <u>shouldn't / must not</u> be late or you will not pass the course.

14. People under 18 <u>had better not / cannot</u> drive legally in that country.

EXERCISE 3 Complete each sentence with a true statement about your life.

Example: Tomorrow, I'd better not _____ *miss my appointment with the doctor.* _____

1. When I go home, I shouldn't _____

2. Students at my school must not _____

3. Students cannot _____

4. Teachers are not supposed to _____

5. Students may not _____

6. To graduate I don't have to _____

7. During tests students must not _____

8. To learn English I'd better not _____

9. Tonight, I don't have to _____

PRACTICE 22 Making Suggestions

EXAMPLE	EXPLANATION
You **could** use a caller ID to see who is calling on the telephone. You **can** have them send you information by mail.	*Can* and *could* are used to offer suggestions when more than one choice is acceptable.
You **should** always be careful of strange callers. You **shouldn't** give out your credit card number. You **ought to** inform the phone company if you receive strange phone calls.	*Should* and *ought to* are used when you feel that there is only one right way.

LANGUAGE NOTES:

1. *Can* and *could* have the same meaning in offering suggestions. *Could* does not have a past meaning in offering suggestions.
2. *Ought* is always followed by the infinitive (*to* + the base verb).
3. Avoid the use of *ought to* in negative and question form. Use *should* instead.

EXERCISE 1 Circle the better modal.

Example: My friend is sick. I (should) / could call her.

1. The teacher said that I can / should write my paper on any subject.
2. He is very sick with the flu. He can / ought to stay in bed.
3. There are so many things to do in this city. We could / should see a show or eat out.
4. You could / ought to follow your doctor's advice.
5. You cannot / should not put your bag down at any time at an airport.
6. All tourists could / should be careful when traveling.
7. You can / ought to go to bed early if you're so tired.
8. She can't understand trigonometry. She ought to / can get a math tutor right away.
9. We can / should visit your parents or your sister.
10. You ought to / could buy your mother some perfume or a new scarf.
11. There is my old friend. I could / should say hello to him.
12. You could / ought to pick the red sweater. You look nice in red.

EXERCISE 2 Write a suggestion for a person who says each of the following statements. Use *can* and *could*.

1. He can't find his wallet.

   He could look in all of his pockets.

2. I want to find a friend that I haven't heard from in 10 years.

   _____

3. They need some ideas for their compositions.

   _____

4. It's my best friend's birthday tomorrow. I need to get her a special gift.

   _____

5. I don't have time to go to the mall to shop for a gift.

   _____

6. We want to study Spanish.

   _____

7. She needs to save money.

   _____

8. I want to improve my spelling in English.

   _____

EXERCISE 3 Complete each sentence with what you *should* or *shouldn't* do to learn English better.

Example: I _____ *should* _____ speak English with my friends.

1. I _____ speak my own language in English class.
2. I _____ go to movies in English.
3. I _____ try to make English-speaking friends.
4. I _____ try to translate every word in English into my language.
5. I _____ get frustrated. It takes time to learn a language.
6. I _____ keep a journal of new vocabulary words.
7. I _____ be shy about asking what words mean.
8. I _____ forget to do my homework every night.

PRACTICE 23 Expectations

EXAMPLE	EXPLANATION
There **is supposed to** be a birthday party tonight. It**'s supposed to** rain this weekend. This cream **is supposed to** make your skin look younger.	*Be supposed to* is used to show that we have an expectation about something. The information may be true or false.
I**'m supposed to** write a paper for my class. Teachers **are supposed to** help students learn.	In these examples, the subject of *be supposed to* is expected to do something.

LANGUAGE NOTE: Remember that *be supposed to* is also used for rules and laws:

Drivers *are supposed to* wear a seatbelt.
We*'re not supposed to* talk during the test.

EXERCISE 1 Harry's doctor gave him a list of things that he expects him to do before his next doctor's visit. Write sentences telling what Harry is supposed to do, using *supposed to*.

Example: (not) eat any candy or sweets

He is not supposed to eat any candy or sweets.

1. eat lots of fresh vegetables

2. get plenty of sleep

3. exercise every day

4. drink lots of water

5. (not) worry about things

6. spend more time with his family

7. (not) feel too much stress

8. take some time off now and then

   _____

9. (not) think about work at night

   _____

10. count to 10 before he gets angry

    _____

EXERCISE 2 Read the information about the recommended daily food servings for a healthy diet. Then write a sentence about the foods in parentheses using *supposed to*.

Fat group   Fats, oils, and sweets: 0 to 2 servings a day

Dairy group   Milk, yogurt, and cheese: 2 to 3 servings a day

Meat group   Meat, chicken, fish, beans, eggs, and nuts: 2 to 3 servings a day

Vegetable group   Tomatoes, spinach, and carrots: 3 to 5 servings a day

Grain group   Bread, cereal, rice, and pasta: 6 to 11 servings a day

Example: (bread, cereal, rice and pasta)

   You are supposed to eat 6 to 11 servings of the grain group a day.

1. (fats, oils, and sweets)

   _____

2. (vegetables)

   _____

3. (meat, chicken, fish, beans, eggs, and nuts)

   _____

4. (milk, yogurt, and cheese)

   _____

EXERCISE 3 Read the following beliefs about certain foods, and write a sentence about each belief using *be supposed to*.

Example: During a special holiday in Japan, beans are thrown in doorways of homes to

   keep evil out.

   Beans *are supposed to keep evil out of the home.*

1. Many people believe that strawberries whiten teeth.

   Strawberries _____

2. Some cultures feel an apple every day is healthy.

   An apple every day _____

PRACTICE 24 Possibilities

EXAMPLE	EXPLANATION
You **may** already know her. This **could** be your lucky day. Some promises **might** not be true now.	Use *may, might,* and *could* to show possibilities about the present. Use *already* and *now* with the modals to emphasize present possibility.
If you enter, you **could** win a prize. You **may** win, but the chances are slim. You **might** win a cheap, useless prize. Do you think I **could** win the prize?	Use *may, might,* and *could* to show possibilities about the future. The outcome is not certain.

LANGUAGE NOTES:
1. Compare certainty and uncertainty about the present and future:
   Present: You are a winner. (certain). You may already be a winner. (uncertain)
   Future: You will win a prize. (certain) You may win a prize. (uncertain)
2. For negative possibility, we use *may not* or *might not*. (Don't use *could not*; it means *was not able to.*) We do not make a contraction with *may not* or *might not.*
3. *Maybe,* written as one word, is an adverb. *May be* written as two words is a modal + verb:
   Maybe you are right. = You *may be* right.

EXERCISE 1 Label each sentence *P* for present possibility or *F* for future possibility.

Example: _____*P*_____ I may leave now.

1. _____ She could leave one day soon.
2. _____ You might not believe me.
3. _____ Our friends may come soon.
4. _____ The basketball game could already be over.
5. _____ We might do that someday.
6. _____ He could be here now.
7. _____ I could go to Florida.
8. _____ The girls may love that color dress, but it's too expensive.
9. _____ The future might already be here.
10. _____ You might not have a cold.

EXERCISE 2 Match each situation with the appropriate result.

1. If it rains during the picnic, __H__
2. If I don't do my homework, _____
3. If I buy a computer, _____
4. If people don't protect the environment, _____
5. If my car breaks down, _____
6. If you play the lottery, _____
7. If you don't study hard, _____
8. If it is a nice day, _____
9. If it snows all day, _____
10. If her parents come to visit, _____

A. you might not graduate.
B. I may go for a long walk.
C. school could be canceled.
D. I could take it to the garage.
E. I might spend a lot of money on it.
F. she might introduce her friends.
G. you could win.
H. we might have to eat indoors.
I. we may lose endangered animals.
J. I may not learn about modals.

EXERCISE 3 Answer each question by using the word in parentheses. Use *not* if necessary.

Example: Are you going to the game? (may) *I may go to the game.* _____

1. Will it rain tomorrow? (might) _____
2. Will they go on a picnic? (may) _____
3. Is your friend coming to visit? (might) _____
4. If she comes, will you go out? (could) _____
5. Will you go back home soon? (may) _____
6. If you study, will you finish early? (could) _____
7. Does the store carry computers? (might) _____

EXERCISE 4 Write *Do you think* questions with the following modals and verbs.

Example: might / borrow your pen
Do you think she might borrow your pen? _____

1. may / have / your attention

_____

2. could / take the bus

_____

3. might / win the prize

_____

PRACTICE **25** Logical Conclusions

EXAMPLE	EXPLANATION
1. a. She doesn't have any money. She **must** find a job. b. He didn't pass the exam. He **must** study harder. 2. a. He won a lot of money. He **must** feel great. b. She knows all the test answers. She **must be** smart.	*Must* has two completely different uses: 1. *Must* is an expression of necessity. 2. *Must* shows a conclusion based on information we have or observations we make. In this case, *must* talks about the present only, not the future.

LANGUAGE NOTE: For a negative conclusion, use *must not*. Do not use a contraction.

EXERCISE 1 Decide whether *must* in the following sentences means *N* (necessity) or a *LC* (logical conclusion). Write *N* or *LC*.

Example: People have heavy coats on. It must be cold outside. _____*LC*_____

1. The library has strict rules. You must return the book on the due date. _____

2. Their car is full of suitcases. They must be going on vacation. _____

3. The test is tomorrow. You must take the test to graduate. _____

4. To apply for the job, you must complete the application. _____

5. They have eight children. They must love kids. _____

6. It's late. I must go at once. _____

7. He forgot his sweater. He must be cold. _____

8. Mary is not here today. She must be sick. _____

9. They must hand in their research papers tomorrow to receive a grade. _____

10. Wendy writes her family every day. She must miss them. _____

11. We don't have enough time. We must hurry. _____

12. You paid your bills for the department store late. You must pay on time. _____

13. The teacher is watching his students graduate. He must feel proud. _____

14. Jill is at work early every day. She must love her job. _____

EXERCISE 2 Use *must* + base form of a verb to write a logical conclusion about the previous sentence.

Example: She rarely takes her lunch hour.
She must be busy at work.

1. He takes the train into the city every morning except Saturdays and Sundays.

    _____

2. She is buying dog food at the pet shop.

    _____

3. They have two basketballs, a soccer ball, and three tennis rackets in their garage.

    _____

4. She has seen her favorite movie 20 times.

    _____

5. He is at the bus stop with a suitcase.

    _____

6. The air conditioners are on in all of the houses.

    _____

7. Ken wears a different hat to school every day.

    _____

8. Sandy has more than 200 CDs.

    _____

9. He was buying cold medicine at the store.

    _____

10. They have many toys in their house.

    _____

11. The businessman is running to the bus at 10:00 a.m.

    _____

12. The girls are happy wearing dirty uniforms and carrying a soccer ball.

    _____

PRACTICE 26 Modals with Continuous Verbs

EXAMPLE	EXPLANATION
This child **should be sleeping.** She **shouldn't be watching** TV now.	Use modal (or modal expression) + *be* + verb *–ing* for a continuous meaning.
I can't reach my friend. His line is always busy. He **might be using** the Internet now.	
We are **supposed to be listening** to the teacher.	

EXERCISE 1 Circle the correct form of the verb.

1. It's only 5:00 a.m. They must be <u>sleep / sleeping</u>.

2. We shouldn't be talking. We should be <u>listened / listening</u> to the lecture.

3. They are going on vacation next week. They might be <u>go / going</u> to Mexico.

4. His car is at the shop. He could <u>borrowing / borrow</u> mine if he wants.

5. Her favorite TV show is on right now. She must be <u>watch / watching</u> it.

6. The weather report doesn't look good. It may <u>rain / raining</u> tomorrow.

7. You must <u>going / go</u> at once to see the boss.

8. No one is at home. Everyone must be <u>work / working</u> right now.

9. They are supposed to <u>gone / be going</u> to London next week.

10. She has an exam tomorrow. She must be <u>studying / studied</u> tonight.

EXERCISE 2 Find the mistake in each sentence. Every sentence should contain a modal + *be* + a continuous verb. Rewrite the sentence with a corrected verb phrase.

Example: They are <u>supposed to be have</u> lunch right now.

They are supposed to be having lunch right now.

1. Everyone is carrying an umbrella. It <u>must be rained</u>.

_____

2. She <u>might be plans</u> a trip to visit her friends.

_____

3. They are sleeping in class. They <u>should being listening</u>.

_____

4. There is no traffic on the roads. People <u>may be taked</u> a holiday.

_____

5. She's not at home. She <u>could be visited</u> a friend.

_____

6. He's buying lots of food. He <u>might be had</u> a party.

_____

EXERCISE 3 Maria is on vacation this week, but she is thinking about work. She knows what usually happens at the office. Read the following statements and tell what *may, must, should be,* or *is supposed to be* happening right now.

Example: They usually have a meeting.   (must)
        They must be having a meeting.
        _____

1. The boss sometimes assigns projects.   (may)

   _____

2. Jim always makes coffee.   (must)

   _____

3. Sally prepares the weekly report.   (should)

   _____

4. George always answers the phones.   (must)

   _____

5. Mary sometimes greets visitors.   (might)

   _____

6. Sometimes Susan doesn't do her work.   (be supposed to)

   _____

7. My coworkers are probably wondering what I am doing.   (must)

   _____

8. Mike occasionally checks the computers.   (might)

   _____

9. Naomi usually waters the plants.   (must)

   _____

10. Peter works on the filing.   (be supposed to)

    _____

PRACTICE 27 Modals in the Past: *Have* + Past Participle

ACTIVE:

SUBJECT	MODAL	(*NOT*)	*HAVE*	PAST PARTICIPLE	COMPLEMENT
He	might		have	been	tired.
He	may	not	have	had	enough sleep.
He	must		have	taken	his medicine.
He	should		have	gone to bed	early.
He	should	not	have	stayed up	late.

PASSIVE:

SUBJECT	MODAL	(*NOT*)	*HAVE BEEN*	PAST PARTICIPLE	COMPLEMENT
He	must		have been	kept up	by the noise.
The noise	should		have been	reported	to the police.
He	should	not	have been	kept awake.	

LANGUAGE NOTES:

1. The only modal that has a past form is *can*. The past form is *could:*
   I *can* speak English now. I *couldn't* speak English three years ago.
2. The past of *must*, when it shows necessity, is *had to:*
   Next week I *must* renew my driver's license.
   Last month I *had to* get an application.
3. For the other modals, we use modal + *have* + past participle to give a past meaning.

EXERCISE 1 Complete each sentence with an active modal in the past.

A. The coach wanted to know why the team lost the soccer match yesterday.

Example: They (might / practice) ___*might have practiced*___ harder.

1. The classmates (could / encourage) _____ the team.

2. The coach (could / spend) _____ more time training the team.

3. The players (should / work) _____ together.

4. The goal (*passive:* should / not / leave) _____ by the goalie.

B. The police don't know why the accident happened, but they have some ideas.

1. The driver (may / drive) _____ carelessly.

2. The drivers (might / drive) _____ too fast.

3. One car (might / try) _____ to pass the other car.

4. An animal (may / cross) _____ the road.

5. A cell phone (*passive:* may / used) _____ by the driver.

C. Mary did not do well on the exam.

1. She (may / not / pay attention) _____ in class.

2. She (may / talk) _____ when the teacher explained the work.

3. She's often tired in class, so she (might / fall asleep) _____ .

4. She also (could / daydream) _____ .

5. She (must / not / study) _____ hard all week.

D. The family probably didn't go sailing last Saturday for many reasons.

1. The wind (might / blow) _____ too hard.

2. There (may / be) _____ warnings about the rough sea.

3. They (may / expect) _____ a big storm.

4. There also (could / be) _____ a problem with their boat.

5. They love to sail, so they (must / be) _____ disappointed.

EXERCISE 2 Complete each sentence with a modal (*may, might, must,* or *should*) + *have* + the past participle of the verb in parentheses.

Example: She didn't come to class. She (not / feel) _____*may not have felt*_____ well.

1. He didn't answer the phone yesterday. He (not / hear) _____ it.

2. My friends weren't at movies last night. They (not / come) _____ .

3. After school, the streets were wet. It (rain) _____ .

4. She was sick, but she came to school. She (stay) _____ in bed.

5. All weekend, we watched TV. We (go) _____ outside instead.

EXERCISE 3 Unscramble each of these sentences. Each sentence is passive.

Example: by the loud music / he / must / awoken / been / have
He must have been awoken by the loud music.

1. couldn't / she / the directions / understood / have / from the teacher

_____

2. you / been / contacted / yet / by the dentist's assistant / may / not / have

_____

3. the assigned book / been / have / by the students / might / already / read

_____

4. by her sister's questions / she / should / have / not / bothered / been

_____

PRACTICE 28 Past Possibility

EXAMPLE	EXPLANATION
Why did the Mayan civilization disappear from the Yucatan Peninsula? There are several possibilities. They **could have been** killed in wars. They **may have starved** to death. They **might have moved** away.	Use *may have, might have,* or *could have* + past participle to express possibility about the past. The sentences on the left give theories about the past.

LANGUAGE NOTES:

1. Compare possibility with *maybe* and possibility with modals:

   Maybe he was injured in the war. ⟶ He *might have been injured* in the war.
   Maybe the battle injured him. ⟶ Wars *could have injured* him.

2. For negative possibility, don't use *could not have* because it has a different meaning. *Could not have* indicates no possible way.

EXERCISE 1 Change these *maybe* statements to statements with *may have, might have,* and *could have.*

Situation: You have decided to study abroad. Your friends wonder why you decided this.

Example: Maybe you were bored with studying in your own country.
You may have been bored with studying in your own country.

1. Maybe you wanted to live in another country.

   _____

2. Maybe you thought it would be fun.

   _____

3. Maybe all of your friends had gone abroad.

   _____

4. Maybe your teacher recommended it.

   _____

5. Maybe you hoped it would help you get a better job in the future.

   _____

6. Maybe your parents suggested it.

   _____

EXERCISE 2 Circle the correct choices.

A. Nobody knows why the number 1 team lost the championship game, but there are several theories about it. The team (**Example:**) <u>should have thought</u> / <u>(might have thought)</u> it could win easily, so they (1) <u>might not had practiced</u> / <u>might not have practiced</u> hard. Someone saw the team members out late the night before the game, so they (2) <u>may have go</u> / <u>may have gone</u> to bed too late. During the game they (3) <u>can have been</u> / <u>could have been</u> tired, and they (4) <u>may not have tried</u> / <u>might not have been tried</u> hard. It's too bad because they (5) <u>should have won</u> / <u>should have been winning</u> the game.

B. No one knows for sure what (1) <u>could have happened</u> / <u>could be happened</u> to the ship that disappeared at sea, but there are many theories about it. One theory says that pirates (2) <u>should have taken</u> / <u>could have taken</u> over the ship. Another theory says that a horrible storm (3) <u>might have sunk</u> / <u>might have been sinking</u> the ship. Yet another theory is that a sea creature (4) <u>could have caused</u> / <u>can have caused</u> the ship to sink. I agree that there (5) <u>might have been</u> / <u>might have being</u> a terrible storm.

EXERCISE 3 Read the statements. Then use the words in parentheses to write about a possibility in the past.

1. The child lost her money.   (could)
   She could have been more careful.

2. They got wet.   (could)
   _____

3. She didn't pass the exam.   (might)
   _____

4. She lost her wallet.   (could)
   _____

5. They didn't watch TV last night.   (might)
   _____

6. He missed the bus.   (may)
   _____

PRACTICE 29 Past Necessity: *Had To* vs. *Must Have*

EXAMPLE	EXPLANATION
He **had to study** for the exam. He **had to ask** the teacher if he could take it early. He **had to leave** school early.	Use *had to* + base form to show necessity (personal or legal) about the past.
When he arrived late, the teacher **must have been** worried. The families of those lost at sea **must have felt** a great loss.	Use *must have* + past participle to make a conclusion about the past.
The investigation determined that the ship **must have sunk** in a terrible storm. When he didn't arrive on time, his teacher thought he **must have missed** the bus.	We use *must have* + past participle to make a statement of deduction about a past event based on observations we make and information we have.

EXERCISE 1 Fill in each blank with the correct form of the verb in parentheses.

Example: He had to (pass) _____*pass*_____ the exam to enter the next class.

1. He must have (be) _____ nervous.

2. He had to (study) _____ every night for several weeks.

3. He must have (feel) _____ very tired every day.

4. He had to (review) _____ many grammar points.

5. He had to (memorize) _____ hundreds of vocabulary words.

6. Because he hadn't done any homework all semester, he had to (catch up) _____ on a lot of work.

7. He must have (be) _____ mad at himself for not studying often enough.

8. The teacher must have (warn) _____ him several times about his poor performance.

9. He must have (wish) _____ that he had paid more attention in class.

10. He had to (repeat) _____ the class next semester.

11. His teacher had to (speak) _____ to him seriously.

12. She must have (recommend) _____ that he study harder.

EXERCISE 2 Complete each sentence with *must have* or *had to* and the correct form of the verb.

A. To enter the university in his country, he (**Example:** do) _____ *had to do* _____ many things. First, he (1. write) _____ an essay. Then, he (2. have) _____ an interview. He also (3. take) _____ three exams. By the time he finished, he (4. be) _____ very tired. He (5. feel) _____ happy when he finished.

B. She just left for a long trip to China, but she (1. do) _____ many things before she left. She (2. get) _____ a visa, so she (3. go) _____ to the Chinese consulate. There were many people there, so she (4. wait) _____ in line for more than three hours. When she got home she (5. be) _____ very tired. When I called her at 9:00 that night, she didn't answer the phone. She (6. go) _____ to bed early. I had called to tell her that a program about China was on TV, but she (7. not / see) _____ it. Then she (8. get up) _____ up early and gone out because nobody answered the phone in the morning. I think she (9. make) _____ her airplane reservations that morning to get a special fare. She (10. feel) _____ relieved when the tickets were booked and she was ready to go.

EXERCISE 3 Read each sentence and make a deduction based on it, using *must (not) have* and a past participle.

Example: Wendy doesn't have her homework. She thought she put it in her backpack.
She must not have put it in her backpack.

1. When Bill got his test back, he jumped for joy.
   _____

2. I saw him driving a brand new car last week.
   _____

3. There were no lights on at 11:00 p.m. when he drove by their house.
   _____

4. She didn't get the job she really wanted.
   _____

PRACTICE 30 Past Mistakes

EXAMPLE	EXPLANATION
He **should have kept up** with his work. He **should have studied** harder. He **shouldn't have gone** to a party every night.	We use *should have* + past participle to comment on a mistake that was made. We are not really giving advice because it is impossible to change the past.

LANGUAGE NOTES:

1. Less frequently we use *ought to have* + past participle:
   He *ought to have kept up* with his work.
2. *Usage note:* When a person receives an unexpected gift, he or she may be a little embarrassed. This person sometimes says, "*You shouldn't have.*" This means, "You shouldn't have gone to so much trouble or expense" or "You shouldn't have given me a gift. I don't deserve it."

EXERCISE 1 Sally and Carlos made some mistakes. For each of the mistakes they made, write what they *should have* or *shouldn't have* done.

Situation A: Sally was late for work

Example: She went to bed very late.
   She shouldn't have gone to bed very late.

1. She didn't set her alarm for the right time.

2. She forgot to get her clothes ready the night before.

3. She got a phone call from a friend and talked for a long time.

4. She watched the news on TV.

5. She read the newspaper.

6. She didn't have gas in the car, so she had to go get gas.

Situation B: Carlos failed his English language test.

1.   He spoke Spanish every night with his friends.

_____

2.   He rarely went to class.

_____

3.   He never went to the language lab.

_____

4.   He didn't do his homework.

_____

5.   He often slept during class.

_____

6.   He never read English books.

_____

7.   He didn't read English newspapers.

_____

8.   He never studied for tests.

_____

EXERCISE 2   Read the list of things George's friend said that George *should have* and *shouldn't have* done. Then write what George probably did that made his friend give that advice.

Example: He should have been on time for the meeting.
He was probably late for a meeting.
_____

1.   He shouldn't have driven so fast.

_____

2.   He should have practiced his English more often.

_____

3.   He should have been nicer to everyone.

_____

4.   He shouldn't have gone so long without exercise.

_____

5.   He shouldn't have called in sick so often.

_____

PRACTICE **31** *Be Supposed To* in the Past

EXAMPLE	EXPLANATION
The race **was supposed to** be on Friday, but they changed it to Saturday.	*Was / were supposed* to + base form is used to show that an expected action did not happen.
You **were supposed to** stop at the stop sign, but you didn't.	*Was / were supposed* to is used for rules that are broken.

LANGUAGE NOTE: Do not repeat *was / were supposed to* with two verbs:

I *was supposed to watch* less TV and *exercise* more.

EXERCISE 1 The doctor told her patients to do these things before they came back for their next checkup. Her patients did not do any of the things their doctor told them to do. Write statements to tell what the patients *were supposed to* do.

Example: Drink six glasses of water a day.   (Paul)

Paul was supposed to drink six glasses of water a day.

1. Get plenty of rest at night.   (Jill)

   _____

2. Go for a long walk every day.   (I)

   _____

3. Take your medicine.   (you)

   _____

4. Eat lots of fruit and vegetables.   (we)

   _____

5. Try to relax.   (he)

   _____

6. Take a day off now and then.   (she)

   _____

7. Take aspirin for headaches.   (I)

   _____

8. Come back for a checkup in a month.   (you)

   _____

EXERCISE 2 Linda got sick last week and had to stay home in bed. Look at Linda's schedule for last week. Write two sentences about what she *was supposed to* do each day.

Monday: Go to Christine's house after work

                Work out at the gym

Tuesday: Pay the telephone bill

                Pick up Jan from the airport

Wednesday: Walk in the morning with Ben

                Have dinner with Uncle Bob

Thursday: Take Grandpa for his checkup

                Go to dance class

Friday: Meet Gina at Pizza Time for lunch

                Go to Sandy's surprise party

Example: Have lunch with Ron   *On Monday she was supposed to have lunch with Ron.*

1. _____
2. _____
3. _____
4. _____
5. _____
6. _____
7. _____
8. _____
9. _____
10. _____

EXERCISE 3 Read the list of things that Bruce *was supposed to* do but didn't do. Write statements about what happened instead.

Example: He was supposed to finish the report.

He didn't finish his report.

1. He was supposed to call customers.

   _____

2. He was supposed to attend the meeting.

   _____

3. He was supposed to work late last night.

   _____

4. He was supposed to take his friend out to lunch.

   _____

PRACTICE **32** Past Directions Not Taken

EXAMPLE	EXPLANATION
He **could have been** a professional athlete, but he decided not to pursue that path.	*Could have* + past participle is used to express a past opportunity that was not taken.
If I had known you were moving last weekend, I **could have helped** you.	A person wanted to do something, but missed the opportunity.
I was so hungry, I **could have eaten** the whole pie myself.	A person had the desire to do something, but didn't.
He **could have been** hurt badly when he fell, but luckily he wasn't.	Something almost happened, but didn't.

LANGUAGE NOTE: Compare *could* + base form and *could have* + past participle:

When I was younger, I *could dance* all night.
(I used to be able to dance all night.)

Last night I had such a good time at the party that I *could have danced* all night.
(I had the possibility or desire, but I didn't do it.)

EXERCISE **1** Read each statement and write *P* next to it if it expresses *possibility or desire not taken*. Write *A* next to it if it expresses *an ability in the past*.

Example: If I had known you were coming, I could have given you a ride. _____P_____

1. As a child, I could swim for hours. _____

2. I could play tennis all day when I was 11. _____

3. He could have come to the party, but no one told him about it. _____

4. He could have become an actor, but he decided against it. _____

5. That summer Sally could read books for hours and never get bored. _____

6. I could have stayed in bed all day, but I had to go to work. _____

7. They could speak Japanese when they were young. _____

8. When you were a child, you could have been athletic. _____

9. When you were a teenager, you could run very fast. _____

10. They could have gone out with friends, but they chose to study. _____

EXERCISE 2 Complete each sentence with the correct form of the verb in parentheses.

Example: The ball could (hit) _____ *have hit* _____ the boy, but he moved just in time.

1. The cake you made was so delicious, I could (eat) _____ it all.

2. If I had realized you needed a car, I could (lend) _____ you my car.

3. She could (got) _____ a part in the play, but she didn't want to try out.

4. They were driving so fast, they could (cause) _____ an accident.

5. We could (stay) _____ at the party all night, but my friend wanted to drive home.

6. I didn't know you were sick. I could (visit) _____ you in the hospital.

7. She could (take) _____ the job, but she didn't.

8. When the tree branch fell, it could (kill) _____ the little girl.

9. If I had known you were studying English, I could (help) _____ you with your homework.

10. You could (be) _____ friends if they'd stayed here longer.

EXERCISE 3 Complete the sentences to express past direction not taken, using *could have* + past participle.

1. *I could have taken the advanced classes*, but I didn't want to.

2. If you had told me, _____.

3. I was so busy, _____.

4. The storm was so violent, _____.

5. _____, but her parents were against it.

6. _____ if I had known.

7. I was so tired, _____.

8. If they had been on the bridge when the earthquake hit, it _____.

9. _____, but I saved some for you.

10. I didn't realize you had no money. _____.

PRACTICE 33 Adjective Clauses

EXAMPLE	EXPLANATION
Children **who watch a lot of TV** have no time for homework.	An adjective clause is a group of words that describes the noun before it.
A woman **whom I met** doesn't allow her kids to watch TV on Saturdays.	An adjective clause can begin with *who*, *whom*, *that*, or *which*:
The average child lives in a household **that has three TV sets.**	Use *who* for people as subjects or objects. Use *whom* for people as objects.
Programs **that show violent behavior** affect kids.	Use *that* for people or things. Use *which* for things.
Children **whose parents are at work** often choose their own TV programs.	Use *whose* for possession.
Mealtime is a time **when families can discuss their lives.**	Use *when* for time. Use *where* for place.
Many kids live in homes **where the TV is on all the time.**	
The information **children get from TV** is not always good for them.	*Whom*, *that*, or *which* can be omitted from adjective clauses.

EXERCISE 1 Underline the adjective clauses in the following sentences. Not every sentence has an adjective clause.

Example: The man whom I met the other day is my boss's friend.

1. We work in a building where there are three other offices.
2. You should come to see our office someday.
3. You could come on a day when you don't have to work.
4. There is a restaurant nearby that has great Mexican food.
5. The people who work in my office are very nice.
6. I'd like you to meet them all.
7. You should drive to my office.
8. Be careful, though. Cars that are parked in the *no parking* zone get tickets.
9. The parking lot I recommend is the one behind the building.
10. I'm looking forward to your visit.
11. Choose a day that is good for you to come.
12. I'll introduce you to the woman whose mother lives next door to us.

EXERCISE 2 Circle the correct word to begin the adjective clause.

Example: I like the person to (whom) / which you introduced me last week.

1. The artist <u>which / whom</u> we spoke to gave us the best price for her work.
2. The electrician <u>whom / who</u> works down the street can do the job for us.
3. The plumber <u>whose / which</u> truck is parked in front installed our sink.
4. The wiring <u>which / whose</u> the electrician installed was expensive.
5. The nails <u>that / who</u> you handed to me were the wrong size.
6. The builder <u>that / who</u> built the house charged a fair price.
7. The woman <u>that / which</u> bought the house helped design it.
8. The furniture <u>that / whose</u> we just bought was delivered this morning.
9. The house <u>when / where</u> we lived was torn down.
10. Do you remember the time <u>when / where</u> I helped you move in?

EXERCISE 3 Write *who, whose, which, that, when* or *where* in the appropriate place.

Example: Right after lunch is the time _____ *when* _____ I usually return phone calls.

1. Many of the workers live in towns _____ there is no bus service.
2. People _____ live far away often carpool.
3. One woman _____ I work with rides her bicycle to work every day.
4. She told me that she had two great bikes _____ she can ride.
5. People _____ homes are close by walk to work, even when it rains.
6. The town _____ I live is close to work too.
7. After work is _____ I enjoy being outside the most.
8. The exercise _____ I get walking every day is good for me.
9. The office _____ we work has a lot of windows.
10. Windows _____ let in a lot of light are wonderful.
11. The area of the office _____ I sit is always bright and sunny.
12. The man _____ desk is closest to mine likes it there too.
13. We have lots of plants _____ were given to us.
14. A friend _____ I have known for a long time usually waters the plants.

PRACTICE 34 Relative Pronoun As Subject

Children shouldn't see programs.   The <u>programs</u> have violence.

Children shouldn't see programs | that / which | have violence.

Children don't get enough exercise.   Children watch TV all day.

Children | who / that | watch TV all day don't get enough exercise.

LANGUAGE NOTES:

1. The adjective clause can describe any noun in the sentence.
2. A present tense verb in the adjective clause must agree in number with its subject:

   Children who *watch* TV all day *don't* get enough exercise.
   A child who *watches* TV all day *doesn't* get enough exercise.

EXERCISE 1 Fill in each blank with *who* or *which*.

Example: People _____*who*_____ work during the day don't watch daytime TV.

1. Older people _____ are home more of the day watch the most TV.

2. TV programs _____ are for children are not on late at night.

3. Shows _____ attract people in their 20s and 30s are on later at night.

4. Some programs _____ her friends watch begin at 11:30 p.m.

5. Her friends _____ watch those programs don't have to get up early.

6. Children _____ stay up that late are probably tired in school.

7. Programs _____ begin that late are not at all suited for children.

8. Children _____ watch those programs do not learn anything valuable.

9. Sometimes programs _____ are on late at night are scary to children.

10. A person _____ reads a lot has less time for television shows.

EXERCISE 2 Underline the adjective clause and complete each sentence.

Example: Children <u>who use computers</u> *learn more quickly.*

1. A school that has a lot of computers _____
2. Families who have a TV in every room _____
3. Parents who let their children watch TV all day _____
4. Research that shows TV is a bad influence _____
5. Movies that are violent _____
6. Internet Web sites that try to get people to buy things _____
7. People who use the Internet to shop _____
8. Some Web sites that children can get to _____
9. A parent who wants to protect her child _____
10. The television that I bought _____

EXERCISE 3 Write a sentence for each of the words given to describe what you would like in your ideal house and neighborhood. Use *who*, *which*, and *that* to add detail.

Examples: bedroom

I would like a bedroom that has a large window.

neighbors

I would like to live near neighbors who have some children.

1. kitchen

   _____

2. living room

   _____

3. street

   _____

4. neighborhood stores

   _____

5. neighbors

   _____

6. a supermarket

   _____

PRACTICE 35 Relative Pronoun As Object

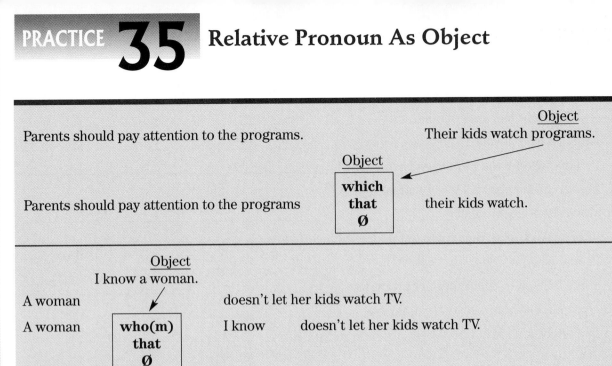

Parents should pay attention to the programs.

Object
Their kids watch programs.

Object

Parents should pay attention to the programs | which / that / Ø | their kids watch.

Object
I know a woman.

A woman   doesn't let her kids watch TV.

A woman | who(m) / that / Ø | I know   doesn't let her kids watch TV.

LANGUAGE NOTES:

1. The relative pronoun is usually omitted in conversation when it is the object of the adjective clause. However, when it is the subject of the adjective clause, it cannot be omitted:
   I watched a TV program (*that*) I really liked. (*That* can be omitted.)
   I watched a TV program *that* had 15 commercials in an hour. (*That* is necessary.)
2. *Whom* is considered more correct than *who* when used as the object of the adjective clause. However, the relative pronoun is usually omitted altogether in conversation:
   The girl *whom* I met at the concert is very talented.
3. In an adjective clause, omit the object pronoun:
   The TV show that I saw ~~it~~ last night was about computers.

EXERCISE 1 Underline the adjective clause in each of the following sentences. Then write *S* or *O* to indicate whether the relative pronoun is a **Subject** or an **Object**.

Example: The school <u>that she showed me</u> was not far from here. _____O_____

1. She went to a school that had about five hundred students. _____

2. They carried umbrellas that were very large. _____

3. The package that I carried weighed a lot. _____

4. The children also wore boots that came up to their knees. _____

5. The food that she cooked last night was delicious. _____

6. A man whom I admire is an elementary school teacher. _____

7. For the children who went to the school, rainy days were fun. _____

8. They got to play games that they loved on rainy days. _____

9. Sometimes the teacher who supervised their games gave them candy. _____

10. The police were concerned about the skateboards which the kids rode. _____

EXERCISE 2 Fill in the blanks to make an appropriate adjective clause.

Example: The English book is difficult. I used the English book last year.

The English book *that I used last year is difficult.*

1. My teacher gives a lot of homework. We do the homework slowly.

   The homework _____

2. I've met many new students this semester. The students are bright and talented.

   The students _____

3. We go to see a lot of movies. The movies are in English.

   The movies _____

4. The newspaper carries international news stories. I read the newspaper every day.

   The newspaper _____

5. I practice English grammar every day. English grammar is difficult to learn.

   English grammar _____

6. The students in my class read a lot of books. The books are written in English.

   The books _____

7. We use the gym. The gym is in the Thompson Sports Complex.

   The gym _____

8. Sometimes we go on field trips. The field trips are always interesting.

   The field trips _____

9. I watch the news on television. The news informs me about current events.

   The news _____

10. You enjoy the food from this country. The food is made from fresh vegetables.

    The food _____

36 Relative Pronoun As Object of Preposition

I don't like the music.   My kids care about <u>the music.</u>

I don't like the music | **that**
Ø
which | ←   my kids care about.

I know the place about which he spoke.   (very formal, almost never used)

I have never heard of the singer.   My child talks about <u>the singer.</u>

I have never heard of the singer | **that**
who
Ø
whom | ←   my child talks about.

I have never heard of the singer about whom my child talks.   (very formal, rarely used)

LANGUAGE NOTES:

1. The relative pronoun of an adjective clause can be the object of a preposition.
2. Informally, most people put the preposition at the end of the adjective clause. The relative pronoun is often omitted.
3. In very formal English, the preposition comes before the relative pronoun, and only *whom* and *which* may be used.

EXERCISE 1 Read each statement and tell whether it is *formal* or *informal*. Write *F* for formal and *I* for informal.

Example: I've read the book that you're talking about.   _____*I*_____

1. The school in which I studied English is no longer there.   _____
2. The person with whom I usually meet is not here today.   _____
3. That is a subject in which I am very much interested.   _____
4. That is a subject I know little about.   _____
5. The country she comes from is bigger than France.   _____
6. The city in which she lives is smaller than Paris.   _____
7. The library from which I got this book is on the other side of the city.   _____
8. I got the CD that you told me about.   _____
9. The friend whom I trust most is Kathy.   _____

EXERCISE 2 Fill in each blank with *who(m)*, *which*, or *that*.

Example: The music _____*that*_____ I listened to last night was beautiful.

1.   The music to _____ we listened was excellent.

2.   The man _____ I talked to in the lobby is my friend.

3.   He's the man about _____ I told you.

4.   The book _____ she was looking at was written by my friend.

5.   The place to _____ I go every summer is three hours away from here.

6.   It's the mountain house _____ I described in my paper.

7.   The person _____ I got the gift from is an old friend.

8.   She's the old friend _____ I told you about the other day.

9.   Her house is the one in _____ I stayed last summer.

10.   You are the student of _____ the teacher is most proud.

EXERCISE 3 Combine the two statements in each problem to make one statement with a relative pronoun as the object of the preposition. Do not use the formal style (*whom*).

Examples: I don't like the food in the restaurant. My friends talk about the food in the restaurant a lot.

I don't like _the food in the restaurant my friends talk about a lot._____ **or**

I don't like _the food in the restaurant that my friends talk about._____

1.   He bought me a beautiful gift. I told you about the gift.

He bought me _____

2.   I have never been to that cabin. They talk about the cabin in the country.

I have never been _____

3.   She had never met that man. You told me about the man.

She had never _____

4.   I've never met my cousin. They spoke of him many times.

I've never met _____

5.   I don't know the answer. You are talking about the answer to the question.

I don't know _____

PRACTICE **37** *Where* and *When* in Adjective Clauses

EXAMPLE	EXPLANATION
Mealtime is a time **(when) families can discuss their problems.** Saturday is the only day **(when) my family eats a meal together.**	*When* means "at that time." *When* can be omitted.
Many kids live in homes **where the TV is on all the time.** I'd like to visit the city **where my parents were born.**	*Where* means "in that place." *Where* cannot be omitted.

EXERCISE 1 Fill in the blanks with *when* or *where*.

Example: The mountains are a place _____*where*_____ many people go to relax.

1. There is a mountain _____ we like to visit.

2. Summer and winter are the times _____ we go there the most.

3. Summer is the time _____ we hike and camp there.

4. It's a place _____ not many people go.

5. It's a spot _____ we often see only animals.

6. Winter is the time _____ we go skiing.

7. The mountain cabin is the place _____ we like to gather with family members.

8. It's a time _____ everyone can relax and enjoy each other's company.

9. The cabin is the place _____ time slows down a little.

10. I feel that it is _____ I can be myself for a while.

EXERCISE 2 Find and rewrite the sentences with the mistakes using *where* or *when*. Write *correct* on the line to indicate correct sentences.

Example: There are many places when I go to read my favorite books.

There are many places where I go to read my favorite books.

1. One place when I go is the chair beside my window in my room.

_____

2. Reading time is a time when I leave the world behind.

_____

3. It's a time when I think only about what I'm reading.

_____

4. I live in a house when the telephone rings often.

_____

5. The house is a house where people are always coming and going.

_____

6. The evening is the time where I usually go to my room to read.

_____

7. It's the spot when I have my big pile of books.

_____

8. It's the time of day where I don't move from the room until I'm finished reading.

_____

EXERCISE 3 Complete each sentence with information of your own. Use *when* or *where* in adjective clauses.

Example: Monday is the day _when I visit my grandmother._ _____

1. My room is the place _____

2. Next week is the week _____

3. My house is the place _____

4. My neighborhood is the place _____

5. That holiday is a time _____

6. Mornings are a time _____

7. Sundays are days _____

8. That park is the area _____

9. That corner is the spot _____

10. This is the time in my life _____

Where, That, or Which

EXAMPLE	EXPLANATION
a. I miss the apartment **where** I used to live.	a. Here, the preposition *in* is not used after the verb *live*. Introduce the adjective clause with *where*.
b. I miss the apartment **(that)** I used to live **in**.	b. Here, the preposition *in* is used after the verb *live*. Introduce the adjective clause with *that*, *which*, or Ø (for nothing).
c. I miss the apartment **in which** I used to live.	c. If you put the preposition at the beginning of the adjective clause, *which* must be used. This sentence is very formal.
a. She lives in a home **where** people watch a lot of TV.	a. People watch a lot of TV there. (*where* = there)
b. She lives in a home **that** has three TVs.	b. The home has three TVs. (*that* = home)

EXERCISE 1 Read each statement. Then use the word in parentheses in an adjective clause to create a new sentence. Begin with "That's the . . . ."

Example: We went to school in that building. (where)
That's the building where we went to school.

1. They ate lunch in that park. (that)
_____

2. They went to a concert in that place. (where)
_____

3. She visited her friend in that city. (which)
_____

4. He spent his vacation in that country. (that)
_____

5. They drove home in that car. (which)
_____

6. They studied in that library. (which)
_____

7. He ate lunch in that restaurant every day. (where)
_____

8. I lived in that house for five years. (that)
_____

EXERCISE 2 Circle the correct answer to complete each sentence.

Example: This is the house that /(where)I was born.

1. This is the apartment <u>that / where</u> I grew up in.
2. There is the store <u>which / in which</u> she shopped.
3. Here is the neighborhood <u>which / in which</u> they lived.
4. This is the hospital <u>that / in which</u> he recovered in.
5. Paris is the city <u>that / where</u> I spent time in.
6. I live in a town <u>where / which</u> people stay for their whole lives.
7. The children love the playground <u>which / where</u> they always go after school.
8. We live in an apartment <u>where / that</u> has three bedrooms.

EXERCISE 3 Write a sentence with an adjective clause for each group of words given.

Example: city / in which / lived

Madrid is the city in which she lived.

1. house / that / lived

   _____

2. apartment / where / lived

   _____

3. country / that / lived

   _____

4. neighborhood / in which / lived

   _____

5. store / in which / shopped

   _____

6. home / that / grew up

   _____

Where, That, or Which

PRACTICE 39 *Whose + Noun in Adjective Clauses*

WHOSE AS SUBJECT OF THE ADJECTIVE CLAUSE:

There are people.

Their only online activity is e-mailing.

There are people **whose** only online activity is e-mailing.

WHOSE AS OBJECT OF THE ADJECTIVE CLAUSE:

Those are my friends.

I've saved   their   letters for years.

Those are my friends   **whose**   letters I've saved for years.

LANGUAGE NOTES:

1. *Whose* is the possessive form of *who*. It stands for *his, her, their,* or the possessive form of the noun.
2. *Whose* is usually followed by a noun or noun phrase: whose bag, whose only friend, whose yellow car

---

EXERCISE 1 Underline the adjective clause in each sentence below.

Example: The language institute is for students <u>whose native language is not English</u>.

1. Students whose English skills need improvement can get extra help at the lab.
2. The morning language lab is for students whose classes are in the morning.
3. The movie night is for students whose classes are finished for the day.
4. The person whose roses are in bloom always has a beautiful garden.
5. My friend whose brother is a famous movie star went to Hollywood for her vacation.

EXERCISE 2 Use the sentence in parentheses to form an adjective clause using *whose*.

Example: There are some students in my class *whose names I can't remember.*

(I can't remember their names.)

1. There are some students _____

(Their native language is Spanish.)

2. Your cousin _____ is very amusing.

(His family lives in Australia.)

3. There is one student _____
   (Her homework is always perfect.)

4. I need to meet with a teacher _____
   (Her class is held in the language lab.)

5. My friend _____ is from India.
   (His conversation partner is from New York.)

6. That is the student _____
   (Her parents came to see her last week.)

7. The student _____ does well in school.
   (I borrowed her dictionary yesterday.)

8. The teacher _____ knows a lot
   of geography.   (His class is going on a trip.)

9. There are the students _____
   (I don't know their names.)

EXERCISE 3 Rewrite the following phrases and clauses in the correct order to make complete sentences.

Example: left his job / has / the man / whose / Jim / name is
   The man whose name is Jim has left his job. _____

1. whose suitcases / there is / that woman / were left at the airport

   _____

2. the man / whose courage / I admire / saved many lives

   _____

3. whose relatives / came to visit recently / my best friend / has been very busy

   _____

4. is playing / whose hobby / there are many students / video games

   _____

5. whose students / have studied / I know / the teacher / advanced chemistry

   _____

Adjective Clauses after Indefinite Compound Pronouns

EXAMPLE	EXPLANATION
Everyone **who received my e-mail** knows about the party.	An adjective clause can follow an indefinite compound pronoun: *someone, something, everyone, everything, nothing, anything.*
I don't know anyone **who lives in Canada.**	The relative pronoun after an indefinite compound can be the subject of the adjective clause. The relative pronoun cannot be omitted.
Something **(that) he wrote** made me angry. You should read over anything **you send** by e-mail.	The relative pronoun can be the object of the adjective clause. In this case, it is usually omitted.

LANGUAGE NOTES:

1. An indefinite compound pronoun takes a singular verb.
2. The indefinite compound pronouns are the following:

   For a person: *anyone*   *anybody*   For a thing: *anything*
                   everyone   *everybody*   *everything*
                   someone   *somebody*   *something*
                   no one   *nobody*   *nothing*

3. In indefinite compound pronouns:

   any = it doesn't matter who / which   *every* = all
   some = unknown / not specific   *one* = *body* = person

EXERCISE 1 In each pair, circle the letter of the sentence with a correct adjective clause.

Example: (**A.**) Everyone who listened to the concert enjoyed it very much.

         B. Everyone listened to the concert enjoyed it very much.

1. **A.** Nothing that he said was true.

   B. Nothing who he said was true.

2. **A.** I overheard something that should know.

   B. I overheard something everyone should know.

3. **A.** Someone lived near you told me that story.

   B. Someone who lived near you told me that story.

4. **A.** That we read everything he put on his Web site.

   B. We read everything that he put on his Web site.

5. **A.** Anything who he wrote was interesting.

   B. Anything he wrote was interesting.

6. **A.** She doesn't know anyone who lives in that town.

   B. She doesn't know anyone lives in that town.

7. **A.** I don't know everyone who lives in the town.

   B. I don't know who everyone lives in the town.

8. **A.** Nothing who you say will bother me.

   B. Nothing that you say will bother me.

EXERCISE 2 Fill in each blank with an indefinite compound pronoun: *someone, something, everyone, everything, nothing,* or *anything.*

Example: _____*Everything*_____ that she knows about cars she read in a book.

1. He doesn't remember _____ that I taught him.

2. I know _____ who is in my class. They are all my friends.

3. She knows a little about _____ that there is to know.

4. There's _____ she doesn't know a little about.

5. Oh, there's _____ that I've been meaning to tell you.

6. He told me _____ that was very personal.

7. Do you remember _____ you saw at the museum?

8. No, I don't. I forgot _____ that I saw at the exhibit.

9. Did you invite _____ who you met to the party?

10. Yes, and I invited _____ whom I just met last night.

EXERCISE 3 Complete each sentence with an adjective clause.

Example: Everyone *who eats this cake loves it!* _____

1. I don't know anyone _____

2. I can't think of anything _____

3. That is something _____

4. He knows everyone _____

5. I don't remember anything _____

PRACTICE 41 Infinitives

EXAMPLES	EXPLANATION
I want **to leave**.	An infinitive (*to* + a base verb) is used after certain verbs.
I want him **to leave**.	An object can be added before an infinitive.
I'm happy **to see** you.	An infinitive can follow certain adjectives.
It's important **to learn** English.	An infinitive follows certain expressions with *it*.

EXERCISE 1 Underline the infinitives in the following sentences.

Example: She doesn't know how <u>to speak</u> English yet.

1. She hopes to go to school to learn English very quickly.

2. She plans to spend a year here studying.

3. She knows that it's important to learn another language.

4. Her parents sent her to the United States to learn English.

5. They learned to speak it when they were young.

6. She would like to learn Spanish after she learns English.

7. I think that she intends to study another language as well.

8. Maybe she plans to be a diplomat.

9. It's necessary to speak at least two other languages.

10. She needs directions to get to the classroom.

11. She will go to the school store to buy textbooks.

12. Her parents sent a package of books to her to study.

EXERCISE 2 Correct the mistakes in each sentence.

Example: He hopes to going to Africa next year.
          He hopes to go to Africa next year.

1. He wants to helps other people.

2. He is planning work on a farm.

3.   He thinks it's important helpings other people.

_____

4.   He has wanted going since he was a child.

_____

5.   He wants to learned about other people.

_____

6.   He'd like assist with the solution to their problems.

_____

7.   He doesn't know how to spoke any other languages.

_____

8.   He expects to learning the language very quickly though.

_____

9.   I'd love go to visit him while he's there.

_____

EXERCISE 3   Use an infinitive to complete each sentence.

Example: I want *to join the soccer team.* _____

1.   I don't want _____

2.   It's important _____

3.   It's not important _____

4.   I'm happy _____

5.   I'm sad _____

6.   I know how _____

PRACTICE 42 — Verb Followed by an Infinitive

EXAMPLE	EXPLANATION
He wanted **to get** a job. He started **to work** when he was young.	Some verbs are followed by an infinitive.
I want to **read and write** English well.	In a sentence with two infinitives connected by *and*, the second *to* is usually omitted.
Everyone wants t**o be given** an opportunity to succeed.	To make an infinitive passive, use *to be* + past participle.

LANGUAGE NOTE: The verbs below can be followed by an infinitive:

agree	deserve	love*	refuse
appear	expect	manage	seem
attempt	forget	need	start
begin*	hate*	offer	try*
can't afford	hope	plan	want
can't stand*	intend	prefer*	wish
choose	know how	prepare	would like
continue*	learn	pretend	
decide	like*	promise	

* These verbs can also be followed by a gerund.

EXERCISE 1   Complete each sentence with the verbs in parentheses. Use one *to* if two or more infinitives are used in each sentence.

Example: They (plan / marry / travel) next year at this time.

     They plan to marry and travel next year at this time.

1. She (intend / finish / graduate) _____ from school in May.

2. They (want / move to / live) _____ in Belize in the near future.

3. They (prefer / live) _____ in Equador.

4. John (expect / be offered) _____ an excellent job.

5. Susan (decide / go) _____ to graduate school.

6. They (promise / return) _____ to visit everyone.

7. Everyone (expect / miss / think about) _____ their friends.

8. They (not / like / say / think) _____ things like that.

Verb Followed by an Infinitive

EXERCISE 2 Fill in each blank with the passive voice of the verb in parentheses.

Example: He doesn't like (ask) _____ *to be asked* _____ a lot of questions.

1. She likes (call) _____ by her nickname.

2. They need (remind) _____ to do their homework.

3. He hopes (offer) _____ the job next week.

4. They would like (take) _____ on a tour of the city.

5. It's important for children (love) _____ .

6. He doesn't plan (finish) _____ with school until next year.

7. She was lucky (choose) _____ for a part in the school play.

8. The dog refused (lead) _____ into the house.

9. It's nice (offer) _____ a cup of coffee at someone's house.

10. She hopes (invite) _____ to the graduation party.

EXERCISE 3 Fill in each blank with an infinitive to complete the sentence.

Example: I hate *to cook.* _____

1. I decided _____

2. I expect _____

3. I forgot _____

4. I tried _____

5. I promise _____

6. I hope _____

7. I am prepared _____

8. I need _____

9. I like _____

10. I attempted _____

PRACTICE 43 — Object before an Infinitive

EXAMPLE	PATTERN
He wanted **everyone to have** a chance to learn English. The teacher doesn't want **us to talk** during an exam.	Verb + object (noun or pronoun) + infinitive

LANGUAGE NOTE: The verbs below can be followed by a noun or pronoun + infinitive:

advise	expect	persuade
allow	forbid	remind
appoint	force	teach*
ask	invite	tell
beg	need	urge
convince	order	want
encourage	permit	would like

*After *teach, how* is usually used: He taught me *how* to ski.

EXERCISE 1 Write if you *want* or *don't want* the person listed to do the following. Change the name(s) to an object pronoun.

Example: Steve and Erin / help me with my homework.

I want them to help me with my homework.

1. my brother / spend time with relatives

   _____

2. my parents / spend too much money

   _____

3. Alicia / relax on the weekends

   _____

4. John / eat in fast food restaurants

   _____

5. my roommate / wash the dirty dishes

   _____

6. my friends / sleep late and miss our class

   _____

EXERCISE 2 Change each of the following imperative statements to a sentence with an object followed by an infinitive. Use the verb in parentheses. Follow the example carefully.

Example: The boss said to his employee, "Finish the project for me."
(tell) *The boss told his employee to finish the project for him.*

1. The doctor said to the nurse, "Hand me the patient's record."
(want) _____

2. The child said to his dog, "Sit down."
(urge) _____

3. The child said to the librarian, "Help me reach the book on the shelf."
(ask) _____

4. The boy said to his mother, "Give me a cookie."
(beg) _____

5. The teacher said to the students, "Read the rest of the book tonight."
(remind) _____

6. Her friend said to her, "Be careful when you travel."
(encourage) _____

EXERCISE 3 Use the words given to tell what the university expected of its students.

Example: not allow / smoke in university buildings
The university didn't allow students to smoke in university buildings.

1. encourage / get good grades

_____

2. expect / respect other students

_____

PRACTICE 44 Causative Verbs

EXAMPLE	EXPLANATION
He **persuaded** people to give their money away.	Some verbs are often called *causative* verbs because something or somebody causes, enables, or allows another to do something.
You **convinced** me to help the poor. My friends **got** me to exercise.	*Get, persuade,* and *convince* are followed by an object + infinitive.
Volunteers **help** kids learn to read. He **helped** people to get an education.	After *help* + object, either the infinitive or the base form is used. The base form is more common.
His mother **let** him play outside.	*Let* means permit. *Let* is followed by an object + base form.
a. No one can **make** you do that. b. Volunteering my time **makes** me feel good. c. A sad movie **makes** me cry.	*Make* is followed by an object + base form: a. *Make* means force. b. and c. *Make* means to cause something to happen.
The teacher **had us write** a composition.	*Have* means to give a job or task to someone. *Have,* in this case, is followed by an object + base form.

EXERCISE 1 Fill in each blank with the base form or the infinitive of the words in parentheses.

Example: The students had the teacher (help) _____*help*_____ them with their homework.

1. He got his friend (go) _____ with him on his trip.

2. Her mother made her (eat) _____ before she left the house.

3. He persuaded his father (buy) _____ him a new car.

4. Her brother bumped her arm and made her (spill) _____ the water.

5. She convinced the students (study) _____ English for another year.

6. All the neighbors helped them (move) _____ into their new house.

7. They let the children (play) _____ until it was very late.

8. The people persuaded the town (build) _____ a new school.

9. I convinced her (try) _____ bungee jumping with me.

10. You helped me (finish) _____ my art project.

11. They had the neighbors (check) _____ the mail while they were gone.

12. Their parents made them (clean) _____ up their rooms.

13. I'll let you (borrow) _____ my car while I'm gone.

14. She convinced us (join) _____ the tennis club.

15. I'll get my friend (call) _____ you to explain the homework

16. Her friend persuaded her (tell) _____ the secret.

EXERCISE 2 Circle the correct causative verb.

Example: His mother (persuaded) / let him to play outside.

1. The teacher made / persuaded us write a composition.

2. He convinced / let us to write about our own lives.

3. He had / persuaded us close our eyes and think before we wrote.

4. The politician made / persuaded us to give her money for the campaign.

5. She let / convinced us visit her at her office.

6. She helped / had people to find money for education.

7. My mother let / helped me borrow her oldest piece of jewelry.

8. She got / let me to promise not to lose the necklace.

EXERCISE 3 Fill in each blank with the base form of a verb to complete each sentence.

Example: The teacher had us _study verbs._

1. He made me _____ the glass of water.

2. His parents made him _____

3. She let her son _____

4. The teacher helped the students _____

5. My friend had me _____ her.

6. His boss made him _____ the project.

7. The bus wasn't on time. It made him _____ late for work.

8. Her conversation partner helped her _____

9. My manager let me _____

10. Listening to music makes us _____

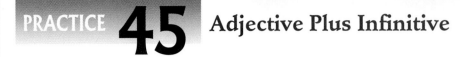

PRACTICE 45 Adjective Plus Infinitive

EXAMPLE	EXPLANATION
Some people are happy **to help** others. Are you willing **to donate** your time? I am proud **to be** a volunteer.	Certain adjectives can be followed by an infinitive. Many of these adjectives describe a person's emotional or mental state.

LANGUAGE NOTE: The following adjectives can be followed by an infinitive:

afraid	eager	pleased	sad
ashamed	glad	prepared	sorry
delighted	happy	proud	surprised
disappointed	lucky	ready	willing

EXERCISE 1 Read and answer each question about Ken and Mari. Use the words in parentheses to answer the question. Use an infinitive in your answer.

Example: What was Mari afraid to do?   (Mari / tell Ken the news.)

Mari was afraid to tell Ken the news.

1. What was Ken sad about?   (Ken / hear the news)

   _____

2. What were Ken and Mari eager to do?   (Ken and Mari / go on vacation)

   _____

3. What was Mari disappointed about?   (Mari / hear that Linda couldn't go)

   _____

4. What was Ken prepared to do?   (Ken / leave very early in the morning)

   _____

5. What was Mari willing to do?   (Mari / get up early too)

   _____

6. What were they delighted to do?   (They / have a vacation)

   _____

7. What was Ken ready to do?   (Ken / enjoy himself on vacation)

   _____

8. What was Mari sorry to do?   (Mari / leave her pets behind)

   _____

9. How were Ken and Mary lucky?   (Ken and Mari / have so much time off)

   _____

EXERCISE 2 Complete each paragraph with an infinitive form of one verb from the box.

| study | ~~have~~ | sit | be | go | hear | know | work | play |

A. Janet is lucky (**Example:**) _____to have_____ the chance to study abroad. She has always been eager (1) _____ abroad. I was not surprised (2) _____ that she had won a scholarship. I'm glad (3) _____ that she will finally have the chance to have her dream come true.

B. When Sam was young, he was proud (1) _____ a member of the soccer team. He was always eager (2) _____ to practices. He was always willing (3) _____ his hardest. Even though he was disappointed not (4) _____ some games, he was never ashamed (5) _____ on the sidelines.

EXERCISE 3 Fill in each blank with an infinitive phrase.

Example: When I was child, I was happy _to help my mother in the garden._

1. Last year, I was lucky _____
2. I am proud _____
3. At school I was surprised _____
4. When I was 10 years old, I was not afraid _____
5. I'm always glad _____
6. I am willing _____
7. My friend is pleased _____
8. My family was delighted _____

PRACTICE 46 Gerunds

EXAMPLE	EXPLANATION
Learning is important.	A gerund is formed by a verb + *–ing*. A gerund acts as a noun.
Learning a new language is interesting.	A gerund phrase can be used as the subject of a sentence.
I enjoy **learning** a new language.	A gerund (phrase) can be used as the object of a sentence.
I'm excited about **learning** a new language.	A gerund (phrase) can be used as the object of a preposition.
I appreciate **being corrected** when I make a mistake.	A gerund can be passive: b*eing* + past participle.

LANGUAGE NOTES:

1. A gerund is used as a noun. Compare:
   Nouns: *Tennis* is fun.   I enjoy *conversation*.
   Gerunds: *Swimming* is fun.   I enjoy *talking*.
2. To make a gerund negative, put *not* before the gerund:
   He's afraid of *not* finding a job.
   Not knowing English well makes my life difficult.

EXERCISE 1 Underline the gerund in each sentence.

Example: They like to run every day, but I prefer <u>swimming</u> as my exercise.

1. Not listening in class can prevent progress.
2. We were having a good time talking.
3. Singing is a hobby of mine.
4. He is enjoying bowling.
5. Dancing tonight is going to be fun.
6. Chess requires thinking and concentration.
7. Drinking warm milk is a good way to relax.
8. The barking was keeping all the neighbors awake.
9. Sleeping is a necessity.
10. Drinking eight glasses of water a day is also important.

EXERCISE 2 Identify how the gerund is used in each of the following sentences. Write *S* (gerund as subject), *O* (gerund as object), *OP* (gerund as object of preposition), or *P* (passive).

Example: They are looking forward to coming to see us this summer. _____O_____

1. I don't like being late for classes. _____

2. Learning English is not always easy. _____

3. I like practicing my conversation skills with my conversation partner. _____

4. I am nervous about giving the speech. _____

5. Staying up late is part of the life of a student. _____

6. I like not having to get up early in the morning. _____

7. I don't like being awakened by an alarm clock. _____

8. Waking up on my own is difficult for me. _____

9. Taking too many exams in one week can be tiring. _____

10. I don't like taking too much time to do my homework. _____

11. I don't care about going to a lot of parties. _____

12. My friends and I like seeing movies in English. _____

13. Going to the movies is one of our favorite pastimes. _____

14. We also practice English by reading English newspapers. _____

EXERCISE 3 Complete each statement with a gerund or a gerund phrase.

Example: _Finding newspaper articles on that subject_ is easy.

1. I like _____. It's fun.

2. I don't like _____. It's boring.

3. I can't stand _____.

4. The school doesn't allow _____.

5. _____ can be challenging.

6. They advise _____ in a safe place.

7. _____ is something I don't mind.

8. I like _____ in my free time.

9. I enjoy _____ on weekdays.

PRACTICE 47 Gerunds after Prepositions and Nouns

EXAMPLE	PATTERN
He doesn't **care about owning** fancy things. He **believes in helping** others.	Verb + preposition + gerund
He was **famous for building** libraries. He's **concerned about helping** the poor.	Adjective + preposition + gerund
He **thanks his parents for teaching** him to save money.	Verb + object + preposition + gerund
He **doesn't spend money going** on vacations or **eating** in expensive restaurants. He **has a hard time saving** money.	A gerund is used after a noun in the following expressions: *have a difficult time, have difficulty, have experience, have fun, have a good time, have a hard time, have a problem, have trouble, spend time, spend money.*

EXERCISE 1 Read each statement and then write a sentence about it using a gerund. Use the verb and phrase in parentheses. Take out the preposition in most cases.

Example: She has a difficult time with her work.

(use / the computer) *She has a difficult time using the computer.*

1. They had a good time at their tennis lesson.

   (take) _____

2. She has had experience with essays.

   (write) _____

3. Sometimes she has trouble with English spelling.

   (spell / English words) _____

4. They like to spend time at their grandparents' house.

   (visit / grandparents) _____

5. He has difficulty when he writes compositions.

   (write / compositions) _____

6. They had fun at the basketball game.

   (watch / basketball game) _____

7. The little boy had a hard time with his shoes.

   (tie / shoes) _____

8. Sometimes she has a problem with her boss.

   (get along with / her boss) _____

EXERCISE 2 Circle the correct gerund to complete the statement.

Example: They don't have trouble (doing)/ do their homework.

1. He doesn't care about <u>to see / seeing</u> that movie.
2. She is concerned about <u>getting / to get</u> her homework done.
3. They are known for <u>being / be</u> the best students in the school.
4. She thanks her teacher for <u>to help / helping</u> her with her work.
5. He has a hard time <u>sit / sitting</u> still to do his work at night.
6. They are interested in <u>learning / to learning</u> another language.
7. He is worried about <u>finishing / to finish</u> all of his work on time.
8. They believe <u>in learn / in learning</u> as much as they can while they're here.
9. They always have fun <u>going / going to</u> their friend's house.
10. He thanks his grandmother for always <u>treating / to treating</u> him kindly.

EXERCISE 3 Complete the following statements using gerunds.

Example: I care about *helping the environment.*

1. She is famous for _____
2. I thank my friends for _____
3. He is known for _____
4. I don't have trouble _____
5. These days I've been spending my time _____
6. He is remembered for _____

PRACTICE 48 — Verb Followed by a Gerund or an Infinitive

EXAMPLE	EXPLANATION
He **likes giving** money away.	Some verbs can be followed by either a gerund or an infinitive with no difference in meaning.
He **likes to give** money away.	
He **started working** last year.	
He **started to work** last year.	

LANGUAGE NOTE: The verbs below can be followed by either a gerund or an infinitive verb with no difference in meaning:

begin	continue	like	prefer
can't stand	hate	love	start

EXERCISE 1 Underline each gerund and circle each infinitive in each sentence.

Example: He likes <u>going</u> to the soccer field after school. She prefers (to go) home.

1. She prefers to study at the library.
2. He hates having homework every night.
3. They can't stand listening to opera music.
4. They began to study English three years ago.
5. He started learning Spanish when he was six years old.
6. She loves swimming and sailing.
7. They will continue taking sailing lessons in the summer.
8. She likes to go to the beach when it's hot.
9. They can't stand playing outside in the rain.
10. You don't like working in the evenings.
11. They didn't continue working in the restaurant in the fall.
12. I don't hate dieting. I just don't like it.

EXERCISE 2 In each sentence, change gerunds to infinitives and infinitives to gerunds.

Example: When she was a child, she couldn't stand taking music lessons.

When she was a child, she couldn't stand to take music lessons.

1. They continued to work on the project late into the night.

   _____

2. She prefers to get up early in the morning.

   _____

3. They like watching old movies late at night.

   _____

4. He began planning his project as soon as it was assigned.

   _____

5. They love visiting their friends on weekends.

   _____

6. She hates to be late for work.

   _____

7. They prefer taking the bus to work.

   _____

8. She'll start to learn how to play the violin next week.

   _____

EXERCISE 3 Complete each sentence with either a gerund or an infinitive.

Example: I will begin *eating healthier foods.* _____

1. The teacher started _____

2. I like _____

3. My friend loves _____

4. We can't stand _____

5. I should continue _____

6. I've always hated _____

7. She prefers _____

8. Most kids can't stand _____

PRACTICE **49** Gerund or Infinitive after a Verb: Differences in Meaning

EXAMPLE	EXPLANATION
I tried **to do** my homework last night. I tried **doing** my homework during the afternoon.	After *stop*, *remember*, and *try*, the meaning of the sentence depends on whether you follow the verb with a gerund or an infinitive.
He loves to work. He doesn't plan to **stop working.** He wanted to finish school, but he **stopped to get** a job.	*Stop* + gerund = quit or discontinue an activity. *Stop* + infinitive = quit one activity in order to start another activity.
He **remembers working** as a child. He always **remembers to help** people.	*Remember* + gerund = remember that something happened earlier. *Remember* + infinitive = remember something and then do it.
He **tried learning** Chinese, but it was too difficult for him. I always write my compositions by hand. I **tried writing** them on a computer, but I don't type fast enough. He **tried to take** a college course last year, but he wasn't old enough to enter the program.	*Try* + gerund = experiment with something new. You do something one way, and then you try a different method. *Try* + infinitive = make an effort or an attempt.

LANGUAGE NOTE: We use gerunds and infinitives in many imperative statements:

> Try to cheer up.   Try exercising to feel better.
> Stop to think   Stop joking!

EXERCISE 1 Fill in each blank with the gerund or infinitive of the verb in parentheses.

Example: When the teacher entered the room, the students stopped
(talk) _____ *talking.* _____

1. He remembers (try to learn) _____ how to play the piano.
2. He tried (enter) _____ the university in the fall, but he was not accepted.
3. She studied English with a tutor, then she tried (teach) _____ herself, but she had little success.
4. He remembers (bring) _____ his lunch as he leaves for work.

5. He had been traveling for five hours straight, but he finally stopped (buy)

_____ a drink and get gas.

6. She had never been abroad, so she went to Italy and tried (live) _____

with a family for a year.

7. They remember (visit) _____ their grandparents when they

were children.

8. His mother always told him to remember (be) _____ kind to

other people.

EXERCISE 2 Read each conversation and fill in the blanks with the gerund or infinitive of the verb in parentheses.

A. Paul's boss was very angry. He had asked Paul to stop (**Example:** talk)

_____*talking*_____ to his friends on the phone while he was at work. He was also

angry that Paul had not finished his project on time. Paul told his boss that he had been working

on the project, but he had stopped (1. help) _____ Sally with her project.

The boss couldn't remember (2. tell) _____ Paul to help Sally. Paul tried

(3. explain) _____ the situation to the boss, but the boss wouldn't listen.

B. Kimi's dream was to learn English. She remembers (1. want) _____

to learn English even as a young child. She never stopped (2. dream) _____

about going abroad to study. She tried (3. enter) _____ many language

schools, but she was always too young. Finally, she was old enough. She stopped going to

school in her country (4. spend) _____ a year abroad. When she left,

her parents told her to remember (5. study) _____ hard and (6. have)

_____ a good time.

EXERCISE 3 Give an imperative statement for each verb. Follow the model.

Example: Stop *driving so fast!* _____

1. Stop _____

2. Remember _____

3. Try _____

Adverbial Clauses (side margin)

PRACTICE 50 Adverbial Clauses

EXAMPLE	TYPE OF CLAUSE
I went to Guatemala **before I went to Belize.**	Time clause
I went to Guatemala **because I wanted to visit my friend.**	Reason clause
I also went there **so that I could study Spanish.**	Purpose clause
I came here **even though I didn't know Spanish.**	Contrast clause
I will go back to my country for vacation **if I save enough money.**	Condition clause

LANGUAGE NOTES:

1. An adverbial clause is dependent on the main clause for its meaning. It must be attached to the main clause:
    Wrong: She didn't come to class. Because she was sick.
    Right: She didn't come to class because she was sick.
2. A dependent clause can come before or after the main clause. If the dependent clause comes before the main clause, it is usually separated from the main clause with a comma. Compare the following:
    I went to Guatemala before I went to Belize. (no comma)
    Before I went to Belize, I went to Guatemala. (comma)

EXERCISE 1 Read the following sentences with adverbial clauses. Underline and identify the type of clause found in each sentence: *time, reason, purpose, contrast,* or *condition*.

Example: He went to France <u>even though he didn't know anybody there.</u> _____contrast_____

1. He got a lot of information about France before he left. _____

2. He went alone so that he could meet as many people as possible. _____

3. He wanted to go because he has always enjoyed studying French. _____

4. His parents had told him he could go if he saved enough money for the trip. _____

5. If he found a job there, he could stay even longer. _____

6. Even though he didn't have much money, he was sure he could find a way to stay there. _____

7. He began looking for possible jobs on the Internet before he left. _____

8. Because he could speak French well, he was sure he could get a job. _____

EXERCISE 2 Insert the appropriate adverbial clause word where needed. Choose an expression for each blank: *before / because / even though / so that / if*

She decided to travel to China (1) _____ she had always been

interested in Chinese culture. (2) _____ her family was Canadian,

she had always wanted to go. She started studying Chinese at the university (3)

_____ she could speak Chinese. (4) _____ she

got good grades, her parents told her they would help her with the trip. Her best friend also studied

Chinese (5) _____ she could go too. (6) _____

they left on their trip, they were very excited.

EXERCISE 3 Match each main clause with a dependent clause to make a sentence. Make the type of dependent clause stated in parentheses.

Main Clauses
She went to Italy
She studied Italian
She will go back to Italy

Dependent Clauses
if she has enough money.
before she studied English.
even though she was only 15.
so that she can visit Rome and Florence.
because her family is Italian.
because she wanted to.
even though she gets homesick.
after she learned Italian.
so that she could get an international job.

Example: (time) *She studied Italian before she studied English.*

1. (reason) _____
2. (purpose) _____
3. (contrast) _____
4. (condition) _____
5. (time) _____
6. (reason) _____
7. (purpose) _____
8. (time) _____

PRACTICE 51 Time

EXAMPLE	EXPLANATION
When he started school, he met new friends.	*When* means "at that time" or "after that time."
Until he started school, he hadn't met any friends.	*Until* means "up to that time."
Since he started school, he has seen his friends every day. **Ever since** he started learning English, he has met many friends.	*Since* or *ever since* means "from that time in the past to the present." Use the present perfect (continuous) tense in the main clause.
He has been studying **for** three months.	Use *for* with the amount of time.
He didn't do any homework **during** the vacation.	Use *during* with an event or with a specific period of time.
While he was traveling on vacation, he had a chance to speak English.	Use *while* with a continuous action.
Whenever he reads a story, he learns new words.	*Whenever* means "any time" or "every time."

LANGUAGE NOTES:

1. In a future sentence, use the present tense after the time word and the future tense in the main clause:

    I *will call* you when I *get* home.

    After he *finds* a job, he *will buy* a car.

2. Use *while* with a continuous action. Use *when* with a simple past action:

    While I was looking for my wallet, my mother found my keys.

    I was looking for my wallet *when* my mother found my keys.

EXERCISE 1 Circle the appropriate word for each sentence.

Eduardo and Marianne met each other in Australia (**Example**) while / when they were studying English one summer. (1) After / Before that summer, neither one of them had been to Australia. They had both come to study English (2) for / since three months. (3) While / When they met each other, neither of them could speak English very well. But (4) during / since the summer, their English improved a lot. (5) Whenever / Ever since they had free time, they went out with their

Australian friends and spoke English. Soon they began speaking English to each other (6) <u>until /</u> <u>whenever</u> they met. Another thing happened (7) <u>since / during</u> the summer. They fell in love. (8) <u>After / During</u> they finish school next year, they plan to get married in Australia.

EXERCISE 2 Complete each sentence with the appropriate time word. In some cases, the tense will determine which word to use.

Example: _____*Before*_____ Cindy went to the concert last Saturday, she had never been to a live concert.

1. She had wanted to go to a live concert _____ she was a teenager.
2. _____ she heard her favorite group on the radio, she thought about going to see them in concert.
3. _____ her lunch hour one day, Cindy heard they were going to play a concert in her city.
4. _____ she was eating her lunch, she decided to try to buy tickets.
5. _____ she got back to the office, Cindy called the ticket office.
6. She called the ticket office several times, but _____ she called, the line was busy.
7. After she had been calling _____ several hours, she finally got through and bought two tickets.
8. _____ the day of the concert, Cindy thought that day would never come.

EXERCISE 3 Complete the following sentences.

Example: Ever since I can remember, *I have wanted to learn English.*_____

1. Until last year, _____
2. Whenever I meet my friend, _____
3. _____ for several years.
4. During the summer vacation, _____
5. When I go home, _____
6. While I was watching TV, _____
7. _____ since I was a child.
8. _____ in two weeks.

Practice 51   **105**

PRACTICE 52 Using the Participle (-*ing* Form) after Time Words

| Before <u>Jim went</u> to France, <u>he</u> bought a book.

Before <u>going</u> to France, <u>Jim</u> bought a book. | If the subject of a time clause and the subject of a main clause are the same, the time clause can be changed to a participial phrase.

The subject is omitted, and the present participle (–*ing* form) is used. |

EXERCISE 1 Underline the time clause and then rewrite each sentence with a participial phrase in the time clause.

Example: <u>Before he studied</u> French, he learned Spanish.

Before studying French, he learned Spanish.

1. After he studies French, he wants to take Chinese lessons.

   _____

2. She decided to visit us after she went to the movies.

   _____

3. While she watched the movie, she ate a lot of popcorn.

   _____

4. Mary got married before she started work.

   _____

5. After she worked for a year, she decided to quit.

   _____

6. She cooked dinner while she was talking on the phone.

   _____

7. After she hung up, she ate her dinner.

   _____

8. The children finished their homework before they watched TV.

   _____

9. Before they went to bed, they read a book.

   _____

10. He read a magazine while he was finishing dinner.

    _____

EXERCISE 2 Read about some of the activities Sally did on Monday. Then write a sentence using the time expression and participle of the verb in parentheses.

7:00, got up and worked out
7:30, took a shower and got dressed
8:00, ate breakfast
8:30, drove to school
9:00, studied in the library
10:00, wrote a paper
11:00, went to English class
12:00, met her friends for lunch
1:00, took a nap in the library
2:00, played tennis
3:00, drove home
3:30, watched TV
4:00, did her homework

Example: (after / got up and worked out)

After getting up and working out, Sally took a shower and got dressed.

1. (before / ate breakfast)

    _____

2. (after / studied in library)

    _____

3. (before / drove to school)

    _____

4. (before / did her homework)

    _____

5. (after / played tennis)

    _____

6. (before / went to English class)

    _____

7. (after / drove home)

    _____

8. (after / watched TV)

    _____

PRACTICE 53 Reason and Purpose

EXAMPLE	EXPLANATION
He was late **because** his car broke down.	*Because* introduces a clause of reason.
They were late **because of** the storm.	*Because of* introduces a noun or a noun phrase.
Since they got caught in the storm, they were late.	*Since* means *because*. It is used to introduce a fact. The main clause is the result of this fact.
They left early **in order to** miss the traffic. They left early **to** miss the traffic.	*In order to* shows purpose. The short form is *to*.
They study English **so that** they can get a better job. They studied **so** they could get a job.	*So that* shows purpose. The informal form is *so*. The purpose clause usually contains a modal: *can, will,* or *may* for future; *could, would,* and *might* for past.
They came **for** a job. They saved money **for** a car.	*For* + noun shows purpose.

EXERCISE 1 Fill in the blanks with *because, because of, since, (in order) to, so,* or *so that*. Some may have more than one correct answer. Don't use parentheses in your answer.

Example: Kim saved her money _____*in order to*_____ buy a car.

1. She worked after school _____ she could earn money.

2. _____ her job, she couldn't go out at night.

3. _____ save as much money as possible, she put her paycheck in the bank as soon as she got it each week.

4. She didn't get to see her friends as much as she wanted to _____ she worked so much.

5. One of her friends started working with her _____ she wanted to earn some money too.

6. They worked the same hours _____ they could go to and from work together.

7. _____ it was so late when they finished work, they usually didn't go out after work.

8. They missed meeting their friends _____ their work schedule.

EXERCISE 2 Fill in the blanks with *because, because of, since, (in order) to, for, so,* or *so that.*

A. Hey, I saw you walking to the station yesterday morning at around 5:30.

B. Yes, that's right. (**Example**) _____*So that*_____ I am not late for work, I have to take the early train.

A. (1) _____ not be late, you have to leave that early?

B. Yes, I do. I know it's early but (2) _____ complete the new project we're working on, we have to come in extra early.

A. Wow! I was up that early (3) _____ I had to take my friend to the airport. I wouldn't want to do it every day. I wouldn't even do it (4) _____ a better job.

B. I know what you mean. (5) _____ I have to get up so early, I'm usually in bed at about 9:00. I go to bed early (6) _____ I won't be tired all day, but I'd prefer to stay up until midnight.

A. Gee, how long is that going to last?

B. Who knows? I hope it won't last long (7) _____ I really hate this schedule.

A. Well, there must be something good about it. Do you do it (8) _____ the good pay?

EXERCISE 3 Fill in each blank with a reason or purpose.

Example: I want to learn English because _*knowing English will help me get a better job.*_

1. I decided to come to this school because of _____

2. Since I didn't know any English, _____

3. In order to improve my English, _____

4. I came here for _____

5. I chose this school so that _____

6. Because of my schedule, _____

7. So that I can learn faster, _____

8. I sometimes talk to my teacher to _____

PRACTICE 54 Contrast

EXAMPLE	EXPLANATION
Even though the team tried hard, it didn't win the game. **Although** it rained, they still played outside. **In spite of the fact that** it rained, we had a wonderful time at the picnic.	For an unexpected result or contrast of ideas, use a clause beginning with *even though, although,* and *in spite of the fact that.*
I like English **in spite of** its difficult spelling rules.	Use *in spite of* + noun or noun phrase.

LANGUAGE NOTE: *Anyway* and *still* can be used in the main clause to emphasize the contrast. *Anyway* is informal:

Even though he has a good education, he *still* can't find a job.

Even though he has a good education, he can't find a job *anyway*.

EXERCISE 1 Fill in the blanks with *in spite of* or *in spite of the fact that.*

Example: Many people choose to work in a city __in spite of the fact that__ they have to commute a long way.

1. My friends had a wonderful wedding _____ a few problems.

2. _____ it rained on their wedding day, they had a wonderful celebration.

3. The wedding pictures were beautiful _____ the rain.

4. They decided to take a honeymoon _____ they couldn't afford it.

5. _____ they only had five days off from work, they still decided to go to Hawaii.

6. _____ the long flights each way, they enjoyed three days in Hawaii.

7. It rained for two of the three days they were there, but _____ the weather they had a wonderful time.

8. _____ their suitcases got lost on the flight to Hawaii, they had a terrific honeymoon.

EXERCISE 2 Complete each sentence with an unexpected result.

Example: We held the party outdoors even though *it looked like it could rain.*

1. Everybody had a good time in spite of _____

2. People got wet even though _____

3. People stayed very late in spite of the fact that _____

4. Many of our friends got up early the next day even though _____

5. Everyone decided to go for a hike although _____

6. People made plans in spite of _____

EXERCISE 3 Complete each sentence by making a contrast.

Example: Even though he has been studying English for 10 years,
he still can't speak English well.

1. Although he studies every day, _____

2. In spite of the fact that he goes to see movies in English, _____

3. _____ although he lived in England for five years.

4. Even though he looks up new words in the dictionary, _____

5. In spite of his effort, _____

EXERCISE 4 Connect the following sentences with *even though* or *although*. Add *still* or *anyway* where they are appropriate.

Example: He was angry. He had a good time at the birthday party.
Although *he was angry, he had a good time at the birthday party* **anyway.**

1. We played soccer for three hours. It was very hot and humid.

   _____

2. The television was on tonight. I finished all of my homework.

   _____

3. She really doesn't like her haircut. She paid a lot at the hair salon.

   _____

PRACTICE **55** Condition

EXAMPLE	EXPLANATION
If we study hard, we will pass the test.	Use *if* to show that the condition affects the result.
Even if we study tonight, we might not pass the test.	Use *even if* to show that the condition doesn't affect the result.
Unless we study, we won't pass the test.	Use *unless* to mean *if . . . not* or *except if.*

LANGUAGE NOTE: In a future sentence, use the simple present tense in the condition clause:

> *If* my brother *comes* to school here, he *will live* with me.

EXERCISE 1 Change each sentence from an *if* clause to an *unless* clause.

Example: He will ruin his health if he keeps smoking cigarettes.

He will ruin his health unless he stops smoking.

1. If she doesn't stop working so many hours, she will get sick.

   _____

2. She will not graduate if she doesn't start studying harder.

   _____

3. If she pays attention to her work, she will pass the test.

   _____

4. You can't learn to speak a forcign language if you don't practice.

   _____

5. You shouldn't try to learn a language if you don't have enough time to devote to it.

   _____

6. If you are patient and practice a lot, you will learn the language you are studying.

   _____

EXERCISE 2 Complete each statement.

Example: You shouldn't eat your dessert if _you don't eat your vegetables._

1. You can't go abroad if _____

2. You can't enter this school unless _____

3. Students can't go to the next level if _____

112   Practice 55

4. You can't borrow books from the library if _____

5. Students aren't allowed to miss class unless _____

6. You shouldn't talk in class unless _____

7. Students aren't allowed to eat in class unless _____

8. Students usually eat at the cafeteria unless _____

9. You shouldn't leave school early unless _____

10. Students are expected to do their homework even if _____

EXERCISE 3 Fill in the blanks with *if, even if,* or *unless.*

Example: _____*If*_____ a person eats fruit and vegetables, he or she will probably live longer.

1. _____ people eat healthy food, they may get sick.

2. _____ children learn about good health at an early age, they might develop poor health habits.

3. _____ researchers are getting closer to finding a cure for cancer, many people die of it each year.

4. _____ we solve some of our environmental problems, more and more people will get cancer.

5. _____ people want to live longer, they must be willing to take steps toward developing a healthier lifestyle.

6. _____ you lead a healthy lifestyle, there is no guarantee you will live a long life.

7. _____ people are aware of health hazards in the environment, they cannot take precautions.

8. _____ people realized how dangerous the sun can be, they would not lie in the sun for hours.

9. _____ you wear sun protection, you can be severely burned.

10. Your skin will be healthy longer _____ you cover it at the beach.

PRACTICE 56 Sentence Connectors

EXAMPLE	EXPLANATION
I would like to visit you. **However,** I will be very busy this summer.	Ideas within paragraphs can be connected by sentence connectors. These connectors show the relationship of ideas.
They wanted to go on the trip. **However,** they didn't have the money. She didn't study at all. **Nevertheless,** she passed the test.	Sentence connectors that show contrast are *however* and *nevertheless*. These words are similar in meaning to *but*.
He is taking five courses this term. **In addition,** he's working three nights a week. I'd like to graduate with honors. **Furthermore,** I'd like to pursue the field of medicine.	Sentence connectors that add more information to the same idea are *in addition, furthermore*, and *moreover*. These words are similar in meaning to *and*.
They wanted to study English abroad. **Therefore,** they went to Canada. They did not get along at all. **As a result,** they got divorced.	Sentence connectors that show result or conclusion are *therefore, as a result*, and *for this reason*. These words are similar in meaning to *so*.

LANGUAGE NOTE: Use either a period or a semicolon (;) before a connecting word. Use a comma after a connecting word:

She was laughing; *however,* she felt very sorry inside.

EXERCISE 1 Circle the appropriate sentence connector in the paragraph.

Example: Many writers say that they have a story inside them to tell.
(As a result) / However they become writers.

Good writers say it is sometimes difficult to write. (1) In addition, / However, they must be disciplined and try to write every day. Writers must let their imaginations run free. (2) As a result, / In addition, they have to have a good sense of structure. Most good writers have practiced the skill of writing for a long time. (3) Furthermore, / As a result, they have become good writers. Some people are natural writers. (4) Nevertheless, / Therefore, to write well is a skill that takes constant practice. My friend decided she wanted to become a writer. (5) Therefore, / However, she entered a creative writing program. She tried to have many of her stories published. (6) However, / As a result, she was not successful at first.

She got many rejection letters from magazines. (7) <u>Therefore, / In addition</u>, she got rejections from publishing houses. She became very frustrated. (8) <u>However,/ Therefore</u>, she thought that maybe she should stop writing. She decided that she loved writing too much to quit. (9) <u>Nevertheless, / Therefore</u>, she decided to be patient and keep trying. (10) <u>As a result, / In addition</u>, she kept trying, and her first story was published last year.

EXERCISE 2 Use the connector in parentheses and the correct punctuation to connect the two sentences.

Example: It was raining. We played golf.   (however)
              It was raining. However, we played golf.

1. She speaks English. She speaks Spanish, Russian, and Chinese.   (in addition)

    _____

2. She wasn't paying attention. She had an accident.   (as a result)

    _____

3. His mother got sick. He returned to his country.   (for this reason)

    _____

4. He was so mad at her, he didn't call her back. He avoided her for days.   (moreover)

    _____

5. He was sick. He came to work.   (nevertheless)

    _____

EXERCISE 3 Complete each statement.

Example: I have been studying English for a long time.
              In addition, *recently I have been studying Spanish.*

1. My friend has been studying for a long time.
    However, _____

2. It's important for me to learn English.
    Therefore, _____

3. Students must be diligent.
    Furthermore, _____

4. My friend didn't study very hard.
    As a result, _____

PRACTICE 57 So . . . That and Such . . . That

EXAMPLE	EXPLANATION
Tokyo is **so expensive that** many young people don't travel there. Her children learned Japanese **so easily that** they became fluent in no time.	We can show result with *so . . . that*: *so* + adjective or adverb + *that*.
They had to wait **such a long time that** they fell asleep. It ended up being **such a terrible flight that** they got sick.	We can show result with *such . . . that*: *such* + adjective + noun + *that*. Note: Use *a* or *an* before a singular count noun.
There are **so many** friendly people at the school **that** you can always find help. There are **so few** students this term **that** the class sizes are very small.	*So many / few* + plural count noun + *that*.
There was **so much** time before the movie **that** they decided to go to a coffee shop.	*So much / little* + noncount noun + *that*.

EXERCISE 1 Circle the correct expression in each sentence.

Example: The weather was (such /(so)) bad that the flight was canceled.

1. It took so much / so many time to get to the airport that they missed their flight.

2. So little / So few people came to class that the teacher decided not to give the exam.

3. It is such / so hot there in the summer that everyone has air conditioning in their cars.

4. He took such / so long to do his homework that he couldn't go to the movies.

5. It was such / so a beautiful day that they decided to play golf.

6. The tickets to the concert were so / such expensive that they couldn't afford them.

7. He studied such / so little that he didn't learn English very quickly.

8. You have such / so a kind mother and generous father.

9. Such / So few people signed up to take Latin that they didn't hold the course.

10. He drove such / so an expensive car. Many people were envious.

EXERCISE 2 Fill in the blanks with *such (a / an), so, so much, so many,* or *so few.*

A.   It was (**Example**) _____*such a*_____ nice day that they decided to drive to the

mountains. They had had (1) _____ bad weather that they wanted to take

advantage of the nice day. (2) _____ people were working that the traffic

was not heavy. There were (3) _____ cars on the road that they got to the

mountains very quickly. They ended up having (4) _____ wonderful day

that they agreed to do it again soon.

B.   Jane has always been good at learning languages. She has (1) _____

good ear for languages that she is able to pick up accents very easily. She also spends

(2) _____ time studying and practicing that it doesn't take her long

to make progress. Jane is (3) _____ talented with languages that someone

suggested she become a professional translator. Jane has (4) _____ other

things she'd like to do that she isn't sure if she wants to become a translator.

EXERCISE 3 Fill in the first blank in each sentence with *so, so much, so many, so little,
so few,* or *such (a / an).* Then complete each statement with a result.

Example: He works _____*such*_____ long hours that
_*he usually doesn't get home until 9:00 p.m.*_____

1.   She is _____ good student that

_____

2.   He made _____ friends that

_____

3.   He had _____ time that

_____

4.   The weather was _____ hot that

_____

5.   The rent was _____ expensive that

_____

6.   _____ people were absent that

_____

PRACTICE 58 Noun Clauses

EXAMPLE	USE OF NOUN CLAUSE
I believe **that all people are good.** He's sorry **that he left his country.** It's important **that you understand me.**	After some verbs and adjectives
I don't know **what time it is.** I don't remember **if I left the stove on.** She forgot **where she left her house keys.**	To include a question in a statement
He said, **"I will return."** He asked, **"Where are you?"**	To repeat someone's exact words
He said **that he would return.** He asked me **what I wanted.**	To report what someone has said or asked

EXERCISE 1 Underline the noun clause in each sentence below.

Example: He said <u>that he would meet me at the movies</u>.

1. She asked, "What time are you going?"

2. I can't remember what time she told me to meet her.

3. He's glad that he came here to learn English.

4. He thinks that it's important to know English to get a good job.

5. They don't know how long they will be away.

6. She said, "Can you leave me the information?"

7. They asked me if I could take care of their pets while they are gone.

8. I said, "Sure, no problem."

9. They are sad that they have to move away.

10. The teacher thinks that everyone is doing a good job.

11. She said that she wouldn't give us any more homework this semester.

12. The students said, "That's great news."

13. He believes that anyone can learn to speak Spanish well.

14. They all think that German would be difficult to learn.

EXERCISE 2 Underline the noun clauses in the passage below. Circle the verb in each noun clause.

(**Example:**) Many people believe <u>that there (is) life on other planets</u>. (1) They think that there must be life somewhere else in our universe. (2) Scientists often ask, "Is there life on Mars?" (3) Some space missions have gone to Mars to find out why there appear to be canals. (4) They say that if they find water, there might be life there. (5) They don't know yet if there is life, (6) but they think that there is a strong possibility. (7) Some people have said, "It's too expensive to send missions to Mars." (8) Others have said, "Well, it *is* Mars. It's expensive to do this." (9) Do you believe that there is life on Mars? (10) Most of us don't know what exists on Earth. Why are we worried about Mars?

EXERCISE 3 Circle the answer that best expresses your belief or opinion.

Example: I <u>know</u> / <u>(don't know)</u> when I'll go on vacation.

1. I <u>know</u> / <u>don't know</u> who the leader of my country is.
2. My parents <u>often ask</u> / <u>never ask</u> where I went last night.
3. My friends <u>don't think</u> / <u>think</u> that I have a good sense of humor.
4. My teacher <u>asked</u> / <u>didn't ask</u> that I hand in my assignment.
5. I <u>am sorry</u> / <u>am not sorry</u> that I took this class.
6. I <u>think</u> / <u>don't think</u> that world peace is possible.
7. I <u>don't remember</u> / <u>remember</u> how much money I have in my wallet.
8. I <u>believe</u> / <u>don't believe</u> that there is life on Mars.
9. My best friend <u>asked</u> / <u>didn't ask</u> how I was feeling.
10. My English teacher <u>said</u> / <u>didn't say</u>, "It's time for a quiz."

EXERCISE 4 Complete the noun clause with *who, when, where, what,* or *that.*

Example: They never remember _____*when*_____ their composition is due.

1. He said _____ he would help us move to a new apartment.
2. She forgot _____ our grammar test will be held.
3. Do you know _____ time it is?
4. I'm not sure _____ left their books here.
5. It's wonderful _____ you won that scholarship.
6. He thinks _____ we are very busy today.

Noun Clauses after Verbs and after Adjectives

EXAMPLE	EXPLANATION
Parents know **that kids need a lot of attention.** Some parents think **that children should have a lot of homework.** Studies show **that early childhood education is important.**	A noun clause can follow certain verbs. Some common verbs are the following: believe forget realize complain hope regret decide know remember dream learn show expect notice supposed feel predict think find out pretend understand
I am sure **that children need a lot of attention.** Are you surprised **that some parents read to babies?** Parents are worried **that they don't spend enough time with their children.**	A noun clause can be the complement of the sentence after certain adjectives. Some of those adjectives are the following: be afraid be glad be amazed be happy be aware be nervous be certain be obvious be clear be sure be disappointed be surprised be worried
An African proverb states **that it takes a whole village to raise a child.** It has been said **that all things come to pass.**	A noun clause can be used after certain verbs in the passive voice.

LANGUAGE NOTE: It is possible to omit *that* from most sentences containing a noun clause.

EXERCISE 1 Complete each statement with the subject and verb in parentheses. Correct the verb tense if necessary. Use *that* before the noun clause.

Example: (I / hope) *I hope that* _____ she comes to the party.

1. (she / often / dream) _____ she is flying.

2. (my mother / complain) _____ I don't visit her enough.

3. (scientists / predict) _____ the Earth's atmosphere is warming.

4. (the student / regret) _____ he didn't study a second language as a child.

5. (they / not / remember) _____ they had visited there before.

6. (the family / decide) _____ they needed a vacation.

7. (we / not / think) _____ our scores have improved.

8. (the students / expect) _____ their essays will be returned soon.

EXERCISE 2 Fill in each blank using the subject, verb, and adjective in parentheses. Note that the verb tenses will not be the same in each sentence. Add *that* where necessary.

Example: (It / be / clear) *It is clear* _____ the earth is not flat.

1. (Early explorers / be / afraid) _____ the earth was flat.

2. (John / be / glad) _____ to hear the news.

3. (We / be / disappointed) _____ we weren't be able to go.

4. (She / be / sure) _____ she left her wallet at the store.

5. (They / be / amazed) _____ when they looked at the stars.

6. (You / be / certain) _____ you will succeed in school.

7. (They / be / nervous) _____ the exam will be difficult.

8. (He / be / happy) _____ his friend called him on his birthday.

EXERCISE 3 Put the phrases and clauses in the correct order to make a sentence with a noun clause.

Example: her story / that / we believe / is true

We believe that her story is true. _____

1. they are coming / is surprised / that / she

_____

2. scientists / an earthquake / will happen / predict / that

_____

3. he / remembers / left the keys / on the table / that / he

_____

4. their team / their friends / that / will win / hope

_____

5. made / they / a good decision / feel / he / that

_____

6. he / is full / tonight / is amazed / that / the moon

_____

PRACTICE 60 Noun Clauses to Show Importance

EXAMPLE	EXPLANATION
They recommend that parents **be** good role models. I suggest that the teacher **explain** this lesson slowly.	After verbs that show importance or urgency, the base form is used. Some of these verbs are the following: advise* forbid* request ask* insist require* beg* order* suggest demand recommend urge* The starred (*) verbs can also be followed by an object + infinitive.
They advise that children under two **not watch** any TV at all.	For negatives, put *not* before the base form.
It is essential that children **receive** affection. It is essential **that you play** with your children. It is essential **for you to play** with your children.	Some expressions that show importance or urgency are the following: It is advisable It is important It is essential It is necessary It is imperative It is urgent The above expressions can also be followed by *for* + object + infinitive.

EXERCISE 1 Rewrite each of the following sentences so that they contain noun clauses.

Example: You should study hard.

It is essential *that you study hard.*

1. You should remember your manners.

   It is important _____

2. Everyone should read every day.

   The teacher recommends _____

3. We should get there early.

   She suggested _____

4. Students should choose their fall classes during the summer.

   The school requests _____

5. Her parents said she must finish her homework in the afternoon.

   Her parents insisted _____

6. We must have our travel documents to show at the airport.

It is imperative _____

7. (You) Call the fire department at once.

It is urgent _____

EXERCISE 2 Change the words in parentheses to make a complete sentence with an object + an infinitive.

Example: I advised (he / wait / for the teacher to arrive)

I advised him to wait for the teacher to arrive. _____

1. I forbid (she / drive fast / in my car)

_____

2. He ordered (we / move / out of the way)

_____

3. She requires (I / pay / an application fee)

_____

4. We urged (he / concentrate on / his studying)

_____

EXERCISE 3 Change the words in parentheses to write a complete sentence with *for* + object + infinitive as a noun clause.

Example: It is necessary (we / feed / the hungry)

It is necessary for us to feed the hungry. _____

1. It is urgent (you / find / money for rent)

_____

2. It is advisable (they / remain / inside during the storm)

_____

3. It is imperative (he / read / Chapter 12 in the textbook)

_____

4. It is essential (she / exercise daily / to maintain good health)

_____

EXAMPLE	EXPLANATION
Before the 1940s experts told parents **that they should be strict with their kids.** They said **that too much affection wasn't good for the child.**	Reported speech is used to paraphrase or summarize what someone has said. We don't remember the exact words because they weren't recorded. The ideas are more important than the exact words.

Sentence with exact quote:
   She said, "I will help you tomorrow."
 	
• Quotation marks
• Comma after said
• Doesn't contain *that*
• Pronouns = *I*
• Verb = *will help*
• Time = *tomorrow*
	Sentence with reported speech:
	   She said that she would help me the next day.
	
	• No quotation marks
	• No comma after said
	• Contains *that* (optional)
	• Pronouns = *she, me*
	• Verb = *would help*
	• Time = *the next day*

LANGUAGE NOTES:

1. Other time changes from exact quote to reported speech:

   today = that day   now = then   yesterday = the day before
   last night = the night before

2. In most cases, reported speech shifts verb tenses to the past of the current form:

   She asked, "Can you help me move in the morning?"
   She asked if I could help her move that morning.

EXERCISE 1 Underline the reported speech in each of the following sentences.

Example: I told my friend <u>that I wanted to leave the party</u>.

1. She said that she was thinking about doing the same thing.

2. One friend told us she was going to be driving home and we could have a ride.

3. We told her that we'd be grateful for a ride.

4. The hostess at the party said she was glad we had come.

5. We said that it was one of the best parties we had been to in a long time.

6. We told her we wanted to leave because we were tired.

7. My friend said she hoped she'd have another party soon.

8. We told her it was a great idea.

9. On the way home my friend said that she'd go back to a party there any time.

10. I said that I could have a dinner party at my house one day.

EXERCISE 2 Change each of the exact quotes to reported speech. Follow the examples.

Examples: My friend called me and asked, "Are you busy over the weekend?"
My friend called and asked if I was busy over the weekend.

I said, "I'm not busy at all."
I said that I wasn't busy at all.

1. I asked, "Why are you asking?"
   _____

2. She said, "I have an extra ticket for a show tomorrow."
   _____

3. She said, "I'd love to have you join me."
   _____

4. I said, "My only plans for tomorrow will be to study."
   _____

5. She said, "That sounds a little boring. You should join me."
   _____

6. I said, "I'd love to go if I can pay for the ticket."
   _____

EXERCISE 3 Change each reported speech to an exact quote.

Example: My friend in Japan called and said that she had some happy news to tell me.
My friend in Japan called and said, "I have some happy news to tell you."

1. She said that she had just gotten a new job teaching English at a university.
   _____

2. I asked her how she got the job.
   _____

3. She said she had seen the posting for the job in a language journal.
   _____

4. I told her she was lucky to get such a good job.
   _____

5. She said that she agreed and that she was very lucky.
   _____

6. She asked me how I was doing.
   _____

PRACTICE 62 *Say vs. Tell*

EXAMPLE	PATTERN
He **said,** "You know more than you think you do."	Subject **said,** "..."
He **said** to the audience, "You know more than you think you do."	Subject **said** to someone, "..."
He **said** that parents should trust their instincts.	Subject **said** that ...
He **told** parents that it was better to feed babies when they wanted to eat.	Subject **told** someone that ...

LANGUAGE NOTES:

1. We *say* something. We *tell* someone something. *Tell* is usually followed by an indirect object.
2. With exact quotes, we usually use *say* (*said*). With reported speech, we can use *say* (*said*) or *tell* (*told*). Again, *told* must be followed by an indirect object.
3. Other verbs that are used like *say* in exact quotes are *add, admit, agree, announce, answer, claim, comment, complain, confess, declare, explain,* and *reply*.
4. Other verbs that are used like *tell* in reported speech are *advise, ask, assure, convince, inform, notify, promise, remind, teach,* and *warn*.
5. *Tell* is sometimes used with expressions such as *tell a lie, tell the truth, tell time,* or *tell a story*. An object isn't necessary in these expressions.

EXERCISE 1 Fill in each blank with *said* or *told*.

Example: She _____*told*_____ me that she would be late for the meeting.

1. I _____, "That's fine."
2. She _____ her friend that he could stop by her house any time.
3. She _____ him that she would be home all day.
4. Her friend _____, "I'll stop by after work."
5. They _____ their friends about the party they were having.
6. One friend _____, "I'll bring some food."
7. Another friend _____, "I'll bring some drinks."
8. They _____ that they really didn't need to bring anything.
9. The friends _____ they wanted to bring something.
10. The man _____ his boss that he would be late for work.
11. His boss _____ that there was no problem.

12. She _____, "Make sure you come in early tomorrow."
13. The worker _____ her that he would come early and stay late.
14. "Brush your teeth and floss every day," _____ the dentist.
15. He _____ the patient to take good care of his teeth.
16. The patient _____ that he liked soda and candy too much.
17. The dentist _____ him to stop eating sugar for healthy teeth.
18. He _____ that fresh vegetables were better for teeth and gums.

EXERCISE 2 Change the underlined verb to another appropriate verb from the Language Notes lists 3 and 4.

Example: _____*declared*_____ The boy <u>said</u>, "I don't want to do my homework."

1. _____ His mother <u>said</u>, "You have to do your homework."
2. _____ The boy <u>told</u> her that he could do it tomorrow.
3. _____ He <u>said</u>, "It's really easy and it won't take me long."
4. _____ His mother <u>said</u>, "I'd rather have you do it now."
5. _____ The boy <u>told</u> his mother that it really wasn't a long assignment.
6. _____ Then, he <u>told</u> her that he'd already done some of it.
7. _____ He <u>said</u>, "I promise I will do it as soon as I wake up."
8. _____ His mother finally <u>said</u>, "Ok. If you promise."

EXERCISE 3 Match the expression using *told* to the correct sentence.

1. _____ The children told him a lie.   a. I told her that it was noon.
2. _____ The teacher told them a story.   b. They said his hair turned blue.
3. _____ The boys told her the truth.   c. We told him 9:00 a.m., not 10:00 a.m.
4. _____ We told him the wrong time.   d. She asked them not to lie again.
5. _____ She asked me the correct time.   e. He taught about the fox and the grapes.

PRACTICE **63** Reporting an Imperative

IMPERATIVE	REPORTED IMPERATIVE				
	SUBJECT	TELL / ASK	OBJECT	(NOT)	INFINITIVE PHRASE
Trust yourselves.	He	tells	parents		**to trust** themselves.
Sit down, please.	She	asked	me		**to sit** down.
Don't be late.	The teacher	told	us	**not**	to be late.

LANGUAGE NOTES:

1 To report an imperative, an infinitive is used after *tell* or *ask*.
2. Use *ask* for a request or invitation. Use *tell* for an instruction or a command. Follow *ask* or *tell* with an object.
3. Never use *say* to report an imperative.

EXERCISE 1 Change the imperatives to reported speech. Use *asked* or *told* + object pronoun.

Example: The coach said to the team, "Try harder this time."
The coach told them to try harder this time.

1. The boy said to his teammate, "Go out for a pass."

    _____

2. The man said to his dog, " Lie down."

    _____

3. Then the man said to his dog, "Stay."

    _____

4. The librarian said to the children, "Please be quiet in the library."

    _____

5. The librarian said to the man, "Check your book out at the front desk."

    _____

6. The police advised the children, "Don't cross the street until you see the walk sign."

    _____

7. The teacher said to the students, "Come to class a little bit early tomorrow."

    _____

8. Her mother said, "Don't talk on the phone too long."

    _____

EXERCISE 2 Change each reported speech sentence to an imperative Change most speaking words to *said*.

Example: The teacher warned them not to be late.
The teacher warned, "Don't be late."

1. His parents asked him not to turn up his music.

    _____

2. Her parents asked her to come home early from the party.

    _____

3. The principal informed the students that school would finish at noon the next day.

    _____

4. The teacher reminded the students to bring their dictionaries to class.

    _____

5. His friends convinced him to go to the movies with them.

    _____

6. Her father taught her to respect other people.

    _____

7. The teacher assured the students that there would be no homework.

    _____

8. His friend advised him not to worry so much.

    _____

EXERCISE 3 Complete each of the following expressions with a reported imperative.

Example: My parents told me *not to talk to strangers.* _____

1. My best friend asked me _____
2. Our teacher told us _____
3. The speaker asked the audience _____
4. Her boss asked her _____
5. Someone I know told me _____
6. They asked us _____
7. I asked you _____
8. You told me _____

PRACTICE 64 Reported Questions

Observe how we report different kinds of questions.

WH– QUESTIONS:

EXACT QUESTION	REPORTED QUESTION
He asked, "What will they do?"	He asked **what they would do.**
He asked, "Where does your friend live?"	He asked **where my friend lived.**
He asked, "Who knows the answer?"	He asked **who knew the answer.**
He asked, "What happened?"	He asked **what had happened.**
He asked, "Why did she leave?"	He asked **why she had left.**

YES / NO QUESTIONS:

EXACT QUESTION	REPORTED QUESTION
He asked, "Is she a teacher?"	He asked **if she was a teacher.**
He asked, "Have they left?"	He asked **if they had left.**
He asked, "Does he know you?"	He asked **whether he knew me or not.**
He asked, "Did they go home?"	He asked **if they had gone home.**

LANGUAGE NOTES:

1. An object can be added after *ask*:
   She asked *them* what they wanted.
2. A reported question ends in a period, not a question mark.

EXERCISE 1 Change each of these *wh–* questions to reported speech.

Example: He asked his friend, "What will you bring to the party?"

He asked his friend what he would bring to the party.

1. She asked her mother, "What time do I have to be home?"

   _____

2. The teacher asked the students, "When do you want to take the test?"

   _____

3. The man asked the woman, "What time is the meeting?"

   _____

4. Joe asked his friend, "What time does the party start?"

   _____

5. The mother asked the children, " Who ate all the cookies?"

   _____

EXERCISE **2** Change each *yes / no* question to reported speech.

Example: The student asked, "Is that woman our new teacher?"

The student asked if that woman was our new teacher.

1. My friend asked, "Do we have to do the homework tonight?"

   _____

2. Her parents asked her, "Are you going out alone?"

   _____

3. The child asked, "Have you seen my mother?"

   _____

4. Her friend asked her, "Did you remember to bring your CDs?"

   _____

5. The man in the store asked, "Is there something I can help you find?"

   _____

EXERCISE **3** Change the words in parentheses to reported speech.

(**Example 1**) The little boy was playing in his yard when he shouted (There's a wolf here.)

___*that there was a wolf there*___ . (**Example 2**) His father ran out and asked (Where is the

wolf?) _____*where the wolf was*_____ . (1) The boy laughed and said (I'm only joking)

_____ . (2) His father got angry and said (Don't do that again)

_____ . But the boy did it again. (3) This time he said (There

really is a wolf here. Please believe me.) _____ . His father came

running out only to find that there was no wolf anywhere. (4) He returned to the house and as he

left he asked the boy (How can I ever believe you?) _____ .

(5) A little while later a wolf did approach the boy, and the boy shouted (I see a wolf!)

_____ . (6) His father asked (Do you expect me to believe you)

_____ , and he went back to his work. (7) After a while when

he didn't hear the boy, he asked (What are you doing?) _____ .

(8) When the boy did not answer, he ran out and cried (Where are you?)

_____ . But it was too late. The boy had been eaten by the wolf.

PRACTICE 65 Present Unreal Conditions

EXAMPLE	EXPLANATION
If I **were** rich, I would **donate** my money for medical research. (Reality: I **am** not rich.)	For an unreal condition in the present, a past form is used in the *if* clause. *Would* + base form is used in the main clause.
If we **could** eliminate all diseases, the world **would** be a better place. (Reality: We **can't** eliminate all diseases.)	Use *could* as the past form of *can*.
If I **had** someone else's brain, I **might be** a lot smarter. If you **knew** English perfectly, you **could work** as a translator.	*Might* or *could* + base form can be used in the main clause.
If he **were living** in his native country now, he **wouldn't be studying** English.	To talk about a situation that is happening now, use *were* + verb *-ing* in the condition clause. Use *would be* + verb *–ing* in the result clause.
If I **were** you, I **would buy** a new car.	We often give advice with the expression "If I were you . . . ."
I wouldn't marry you **even if** you **were** the last person on earth.	You can use *even if* and *unless* in the condition clause.

EXERCISE 1 Fill in each blank with the correct form of the verb in parentheses. Use *would* or *could* in the main clause.

Example: I don't speak Chinese. If I (speak) _____*spoke*_____ Chinese, I (try) _____*would try*_____ to live in China for a couple of years.

1. I am not a doctor. If I (be) _____ a doctor, I (work) _____ in a developing country.

2. If she (can) _____ practice the piano more, she (be) _____ very good at it.

3. You didn't pass the test. If I (be) _____ you, I (ask) _____ the teacher to let me take it again.

4. I have to go to work every day. If I (not / have to) _____ go to work every day, I (take) _____ a trip around the world.

5. If she (have) _____ relatives living here, they (can) _____ help her out.

6. If many environmental problems (can) _____ be solved, maybe fewer people (get) _____ cancer.

7. I am not hungry. If I (be) _____ hungry, I (eat) _____ the whole pizza myself.

8. If he (know) _____ me better, he (know) _____ that I was just joking.

9. If they (be) _____ here, what (say) _____ they _____?

EXERCISE 2 Complete each statement below with your own information.

Example: If I were a millionaire,
I would buy a new car and a house for my family.

1. If I were fluent in English,

   _____

2. If I could see the future,

   _____

3. If I could call my friend right now,

   _____

4. If I could take a vacation right now,

   _____

5. If I found a lot of money in the street,

   _____

PRACTICE 66 Implied Conditions

EXAMPLE	EXPLANATION
I **would** never lie to a friend. **Would** you jump in the water to save a drowning person?	Sometimes the condition is implied, not stated. In these **examples,** the implication is "if you had the possibility" or "if the opportunity presented itself."
Would you **want** to travel to the moon? I **wouldn't want** to live in Alaska, **would** you?	*Would want* is used to present hypothetical situations.
Yes, I **would want** to be a doctor. **or** Yes, I **would.** No, I **would not / never want** to be a cowboy. **or** No, I **wouldn't.**	*Yes / no* answers to *Would you want . . .* questions.

EXERCISE 1 Make a question with *Would you want* + infinitive or *Would you* + verb. Use correct punctuation. Answer your question with a short answer.

Example: be an astronaut

Would you want to be an astronaut?   _No, I wouldn't._

1. climb Mt. Everest

   _____   _____

2. try jumping from a plane with a parachute

   _____   _____

3. enter a burning building to save someone

   _____   _____

4. lend your best friend money

   _____   _____

EXERCISE 2 Answer each of the following questions with *Yes* or *No* plus a complete answer.

Example: Would you lie to your parents?

No, I would never lie to my parents.

1. Would you want to become famous?

   _____

2. Would you want to live in another country for the rest of your life?

   _____

3. Would you tell the teacher if you saw someone cheating on a test?

_____

4. Would you want to be a millionaire?

_____

EXERCISE 3 Write a list of five things that you *would never do*.

Example: *I would never eat candy for breakfast.*

1. _____
2. _____
3. _____
4. _____
5. _____

EXERCISE 4 Answer each of the following using an implied condition in a complete sentence.

Example: What would you do if you saw someone stealing jewelry in a store?
   If I saw someone stealing jewelry in a store, I would tell the manager.

1. What would you do if your best friend took something from you without asking?

   _____

2. What would you do if you forgot to do your homework?

   _____

3. What would you do if you didn't have to study English?

   _____

4. What would you do if you saw someone cheating on an exam?

   _____

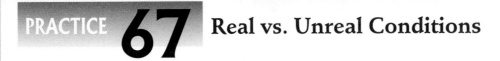

PRACTICE 67   Real vs. Unreal Conditions

EXAMPLE	EXPLANATION
I'm applying for a job in Toronto. If I **get** the job, I **will move** there soon.	These are real possibilities for the future. *If* + simple present, future.
If I **could fly,** I'd **feel** free. If he **had** free time, he **would take** a vacation.	These are not plans. They are just hypothetical situations. *If* + past, *would* + base form.

EXERCISE 1 Read each of the statements below and write *R* (real possibility) or *U* (unreal or hypothetical situation).

Example: _____*U*_____ If I could run as fast as a cheetah, I wouldn't need a car.

1. _____ If it rains, I won't bother to walk to the store.
2. _____ If I had a big car, I'd take all my friends with me to the movies.
3. _____ If he had a bigger apartment, he could have the class party.
4. _____ If we finish work early, we'll go shopping.
5. _____ If I had known you didn't know each other, I would have introduced you.
6. _____ If I remember her address, I'll give you a call.
7. _____ If my friend had Internet access, she could check the Web site I told you about.
8. _____ If she gets a new TV, we'll watch the next video at her house.

EXERCISE 2 Fill in each blank with the correct form of the verb in parentheses.

Example: If I (be) _____*were*_____ at home right now, I (take) _____*would take*_____ a short nap.

1. The course may finish early. If this course (finish) _____ early, I (take) _____ a short vacation.
2. It's raining now. If the rain (stop) _____, I (walk) _____ to my friend's house for a visit.
3. Her parents might give her some money. If her parents (give) _____ her some money, she (buy) _____ a new car.
4. She can't sing well. If she (sing) _____ well, she (join) _____ the school choir.

5. He doesn't have any free time this week. If he (have) _____ any free time this week, he (visit) _____ his friends.

6. His friend may call him. If his friend (call) _____, he (go) _____ to the movies with him.

7. If I (be) _____ you, I (practice) _____ speaking to an English speaker every day.

8. I don't have a dog. If I (have) _____ a dog, I (run) _____ with him every day.

9. The weather may clear up. If the weather (clear up) _____, we (drive) _____ to the beach.

EXERCISE 3 Complete each statement by writing the letter of the clause that best matches the first clause.

1. ___j___ If my friend wants a tour,   a. I'll tell you the directions.

2. _____ I'd take a long trip   b. I would pass my math tests easily.

3. _____ If I remember how to drive there,   c. I would get a job as a translator.

4. _____ If I see my friend today,   d. if I find out what time the party starts.

5. _____ If I were a genius,   e. I'd give some to you, of course.

6. _____ I'd tell a secret only   f. if I had enough time and money to go.

7. _____ I'll let you know   g. I'll tell her you said "Hello!"

8. _____ If I had money to give away,   h. if you wouldn't tell anyone.

9. _____ If I could speak five languages,   i. I'll take college-level English next term.

10. _____ If I pass my next English test,   j. I will take him to my favorite places.

11. _____ I would sing that song,   k. I would buy my family a new home.

12. _____ If I had the money,   l. if I knew the words to it.

For an unreal condition in the past, the past perfect tense is used in the *if* clause. *Would have* + past participle is used in the main clause.

If she **had known** about the problems that were going to happen,	she **wouldn't have** agreed to take the job.
If they **hadn't gotten** sick,	they **would have attended** many more classes.

Might or *could* can also be used in the main clause of an unreal condition in the past.

If I **had studied** biology in high school,	I **could have taken** advanced biology now.
If they **had stayed** any longer,	they **might have been** late for work.

LANGUAGE NOTES:

1. In the *if* clause, use *had been able to* for the past perfect tense of *could:*
   If we *had been able to* make more money, we would have gone on vacation.
2. A noun clause can be used within an *if* clause. Use past forms in a noun clause:
   If I had known *that you were going to come to the party*, I would have given you a ride.

 EXERCISE 1 Fill in each blank with the correct form of the verb in parentheses to complete the unreal condition in the past. Use the modal provided.

Example: It rained. We didn't go on the picnic. If it hadn't rained, we (would / go)
_____*would have gone*_____ on the picnic.

1. She was sick. She didn't attend school. She could have attended school if she (not / be)
   _____ sick.

2. He drove too fast. He was in an accident. He (might / not / be) _____
   in an accident if he hadn't driven so fast.

3. The teacher made him stay after school. If (do) _____ his homework,
   the teacher (would / not / make) _____ him stay after school.

4. She couldn't play the piano well. If she had had more time to practice, she (could / play)
   _____ the piano well.

5. They were not at home when the fire started. If they had been home when the fire started,
   they (might / be) _____ in danger.

EXERCISE 2 Fill in each blank with the word in parentheses to complete the unreal condition in the past.

Example: If she (not / made) _____had not made_____ plans already, she (come)
_____would have come_____ to the party.

1. I (give) _____ you a ride if I (know) _____
    that your car was in the garage.

2. If he (study) _____ harder, he (be able) _____
    to go to the school of his choice.

3. I (not / read) _____ that book if she (not / recommend)
    _____ it.

4. If he (realize) _____ the difficulty of the project, he (not / agree)
    _____ to do it.

5. She (not / take) _____ the job, if she (known)
    _____ that the boss was so difficult to work with.

6. If her parents (not / move) _____ to this country, she (be born)
    _____ in Greece.

7. If the car (not / stop) _____ in time, the child (be)
    _____ badly injured.

8. I (stay) _____ longer if I (have) _____ the
    time off from work.

PRACTICE 69 Wishes

TIME	REAL SITUATION	WISH STATEMENT
Present	I **am** not young.	I wish I **were** younger.
	I **am not working.**	I wish **I were working.**
	Children **can't stay** up late.	They wish they **could stay up** late.
Past	I **ate** too much, and now I feel sick.	I wish **I hadn't eaten** so much.
	I **didn't meet** you 10 years ago.	I wish I **had met** you 10 years ago.
	I **couldn't come** to the party.	I wish I **could have come** to the party.

LANGUAGE NOTES:

1. We often wish for things that are not real or true at the time of the wish. The verb after *wish* is like the verb in a clause of unreal condition:

    If she *were* happy, I'd be happy. ⟶ I wish she *were* happy.

2. If the real situation uses *could*, use *could have* + past participle after *wish*:

    I *couldn't* go. ⟶ I wish I *could have gone*.

3. With *be*, *were* is the correct form for all subjects in wish statements. In informal conversation, however, you will often hear Americans use *was* with *I*, *he*, *she*, and *it*.

EXERCISE 1 Complete each sentence with a wish about the present.

Example: She can't speak Chinese. She wishes she _____*could speak*_____ Chinese.

1. She doesn't have a job. She wishes she _____ a job.

2. He's not on the team. He wishes he _____ on the team.

3. Their parents won't let them go. They wish their parents _____ .

4. I am not going on vacation. I wish I _____ on vacation.

5. I can't stay awake for the movie. I wish I _____ for the movie.

6. They don't study hard. They wish they _____ hard.

7. She cannot sing very well. She wishes she _____ very well.

8. He is not very athletic. He wishes he _____ athletic.

9. They spend too much money shopping. They wish they (not) _____ so much money shopping.

10. They didn't eat enough for breakfast. They wish they _____ more.

EXERCISE **2** Complete the sentence to make a wish about the past.

Example: Bill didn't travel when he was young.

He wishes he _____*had traveled*_____ when he was young.

1. Sally didn't have any sisters.

She wishes she _____ some sisters.

2. She lost her bracelet.

She wishes she (not) _____ her favorite bracelet.

3. He forgot about his appointment.

He wishes he (not) _____ about his appointment.

4. She didn't leave a message for her friend, so her friend couldn't call her back.

She wishes she _____ a message for her friend.

5. Her parents didn't let her go to the party.

She wishes her parents _____ to the party.

EXERCISE **3** Fill in each blank to complete each sentence. Make a wish based on the sentence.

Example: I couldn't dance at the party.

I wish *I could have danced.*

1. If my family were rich, I'd be rich.

I wish _____

2. I didn't know the answers on the exam.

I wish _____

3. If you knew math, you could have helped me.

I wish _____

4. They weren't laughing at my jokes.

I wish _____

5. If I were athletic, I'd join a volleyball team.

I wish _____

6. If her mother lived nearby, she could see her more often.

She wishes _____

Wishes

Practice 69   **141**

PRACTICE 70 Wish for Desired Changes

EXAMPLE	EXPLANATION
I wish my parents **would visit** me.	I want them to visit.
I wish they **wouldn't make** so much noise.	I want them to make less noise.
I wish you **would visit** me more often.	I want you to visit me more often.
I wish you **would cut** your hair.	I want you to cut your hair.

LANGUAGE NOTE: *Would* + base form is used after *wish* to show that a person wants something different to happen. The speaker can wish for something good to happen or something bad to stop. *Wish* without *would* is not a desire for change but an expression of discontent with the present situation. Compare these sentences with *wish*:

> I wish my parents *would visit* me. (I want them to visit me.)
> I wish I *were* younger. (I'm unhappy that I'm not younger.)

EXERCISE 1 Write *change* for statements that express a desire for change. Write *discontent* for expressions of unhappiness with the way things are.

Example: _____*discontent*_____ I wish my teacher were an easy grader.

1. _____ I wish my best friend would learn to drive.
2. _____ I wish my classmates would stop being silly.
3. _____ I wish my relatives were living nearer to me.
4. _____ I wish every country were at peace.
5. _____ I wish my family would send me money.
6. _____ I wish this school would change the rules.
7. _____ I wish my neighbors were quieter.
8. _____ I wish my city would clean up the garbage.
9. _____ I wish the world were not polluted.
10. _____ I wish English grammar were easier.

EXERCISE 2 Fill in each blank to show a desire for something to happen or change.

Example: The neighbor's dog is barking. I wish the dog _____*would stop barking.*_____

1. It's pouring rain. I wish it _____ raining.

2. They don't want to come to my party. I wish they _____ to my party.

3. I want her to help me with my work. I wish she _____ me with my work.

4. She can't come to visit me this summer. I wish she _____ to visit me this summer.

5. The workers are banging on the walls. I wish they _____ on the walls.

6. The teacher is playing the tape too loud. I wish she _____ the tape so loud.

7. My friends aren't coming by after work. I wish my friends _____ after work.

8. My favorite teacher is retiring this year. I wish my favorite teacher _____ this year.

9. I want you to tell me what really happened. I wish you _____ me what really happened.

EXERCISE 3 Sally would like some things to change in her life. Read each statement about what Sally *does* and *does not want* and then write a sentence with *wish* to express a desire for change.

Example: I want my neighbors to stop mowing their lawn on Saturday morning.
I wish my neighbors would stop mowing their lawn on Saturday morning.

1. I want someone to build a swimming pool in my yard.

   _____

2. I want my sister to start picking up after herself.

   _____

3. I want my phone to stop ringing constantly.

   _____

4. I want someone to help me clean my room once a week.

   _____

5. I want someone to do the laundry.

   _____

More Grammar Practice 3

Copyright 2001 Heinle, Cengage Learning.

For permission to use material from this text or product,
submit all requests online at **cengage.com/permissions**
Further permissions questions can be mailed to
permissionrequest@cengage.com

ISBN 13: 978-0-8384-1947-2
ISBN 10: 0-8384-1947-X

Heinle
25 Thomson Place
Boston, MA 02210
USA

Cengage Learning products are represented in Canada by Nelson Education, Ltd.

Visit Heinle online at **elt.heinle.com**
Visit our corporate website at **cengage.com**

Printed in Canada
9 10 11 12 12 11 10 09 08